HIDING

from

REALITY

HIDING

from

REALITY

*my story of love, loss,
and finding the courage within*

Taylor Armstrong

GALLERY BOOKS

New York   London   Toronto   Sydney   New Delhi

NOTE TO READERS:
Names and identifying details of some of the people portrayed in this book have been changed.

 Gallery Books
A Division of Simon & Schuster, Inc.
1230 Avenue of the Americas
New York, NY 10020

First Gallery Books hardcover edition February 2012

GALLERY BOOKS and colophon are registered trademarks of Simon & Schuster, Inc.

For information about special discounts for bulk purchases, please contact Simon & Schuster Special Sales at 1-866-506-1949 or business@simonandschuster.com.

The Simon & Schuster Speakers Bureau can bring authors to your live event. For more information or to book an event contact the Simon & Schuster Speakers Bureau at 1-866-248-3049 or visit our website at www.simonspeakers.com.

Designed by Jaime Putorti

Manufactured in the United States of America

10 9 8 7 6 5 4 3 2 1

Library of Congress Cataloging-in-Publication Data is available.

ISBN 978-1-4516-7771-3
ISBN 978-1-4516-7772-0 (ebook)

For Kennedy.
You are my greatest gift and I am so blessed
to have you as my daughter. I love you more
than anything in the world, in space, and in
spaceships. The cycle stops with you.

Contents

Prologue

I was lying under a black blanket in the back of my Escalade. My heart raced as my assistant, Julie, backed out of the garage and tore through my Bel Air neighborhood, trying to outrun the paparazzi who had been camped out at my house for the two weeks since August 15, 2011, when we'd found the body of my husband, Russell Armstrong, following his suicide.

How did I get here? I thought.

My husband, and the father of our child, was dead. I had been able to sneak out of my house only three times since the discovery, and then, only to plan and attend his cremation and funeral service at Forest Lawn Cemetery in the Hollywood Hills. Since then I had tried to return to Forest Lawn to intern his ashes, but the media crush had been too intense for me to do so, and his internment had been postponed indefinitely.

I needed to put Russell in his final resting place so I could start to feel some closure after what had been an excruciatingly difficult year, most of which I had spent trying to hide the reality of my life from the cameras taping my reality television show *The Real Housewives of Beverly Hills*. And now I found myself literally hiding from the paparazzi, who couldn't seem to get enough of the tragedy that had consumed my life. I'd spent those past two weeks inside my house; I was surrounded by attorneys and advisers, grieving family members and friends, trying to process my loss and make it manageable for my five-year-old daughter, Kennedy, while also trying to manage the financial and legal fallout of Russell's death.

With Kennedy now staying at my mother's house in Orange County, I had decided that Julie and I should go to Palm Desert for a few days of fresh air without the fear of being photographed. I felt such relief as we got far enough away from the city that I could climb out from under the blanket, scramble into the front seat, and ride comfortably as a passenger, like a normal person.

And then, several hours later, as we pulled up to our hotel, I realized that it would take much more than laying Russell to rest to give me anything like closure. I had spent a weekend at this same hotel earlier in the summer with Russell and Kennedy, and the memories came rushing back. That trip had been in the days leading up to my fortieth birthday, when Russell hit me so hard he gave me an orbital fracture beneath my right eye that required reparative surgery; before I told him he needed to move out; before we began the process of divorcing and trying to figure out how we could still be a family for Kennedy and Russell's two sons, even if we weren't married; before he hung himself.

I had hoped that getting away from the demands of my life

in the city for a few days would help me to shake the sick, lost feeling that I'd had inside since Russell died. I knew that part of it was shock at the sudden and violent nature of his death just when I had thought everything in our lives was starting to improve, and that part of it was the sadness of losing someone I had loved so much. But I was also beginning to understand just how complicated my grieving process was going to be. There was so much to come to terms with.

I was alone. For the first time since Valentine's Day 2005, Russell wasn't in control anymore, and I was left making decisions that meant survival for my daughter, Kennedy, and me. The terrible truth was that I felt lost without the control that Russell had imposed on me for the nearly six years we were married. Disturbingly, I had found something comforting about having someone tell me who to talk to, how to behave, what to wear, and what to do. Now there was no one controlling the outcomes, or anything else in my life, and I found that making my own decisions was a burden I wasn't prepared for. In some ways I missed the abuse. I missed the pain. Not because I liked feeling any of that, but because it was the life I had become accustomed to, and now it was part of everything familiar that was gone. Then, in the depths of my despair, I discovered a strength I wasn't aware I had. As I cleaned up the mess left by a man I had come to realize I never really knew, beneath all of the rubble, I found myself. I found the courage to step forward and let my voice be heard. And for the first time in my life, I actually started to like myself. I started to live, love, and breathe the air without the stifling oppression that had dominated my life with Russell.

But it wasn't easy. And I realized that I felt this way even though I had so much going for me—the best psychiatrist money could buy, who had made himself available to me around the clock throughout my separation and since Russell's death; the support of the 1736 Family Crisis Center, a battered-women's shelter at which I had volunteered for almost as long as I'd been with Russell; the love of so many family members and friends; the support of the millions of fans of *The Real Housewives of Beverly Hills*; the incredible opportunity that the show's popularity gave me to communicate with others in my time of greatest need. I thought of the 4.8 million American women who are abused each year, and how many of them do not have anything close to the resources I had available to me. If recovery was *this* hard for me—a college-educated woman who lived in Beverly Hills and was fortunate enough to have means, and friends, and access to support—it must be excruciatingly difficult for others. I thought of how many of these women, like me, had witnessed domestic violence in their home growing up and went on to perpetuate the cycle as adults. I wanted to help them by telling my story and by shining the spotlight I had been given on the issues we all faced. I wanted to explain that I understood why 80 percent of battered women never file a police report or seek medical treatment, because I was one of those women *until* my husband injured me so badly that I finally felt justified in telling him to get out. I wanted to show them that although I had eventually found the courage to tell my husband he had to leave, the psychological fallout of his years of abuse continued to haunt me.

The longer I had stayed in that relationship, the more damaging it had been to my self-esteem, and the greater my level of denial had to be every day.

Maybe I could help other women to leave sooner. And when they did get out, maybe I could make their healing process easier for them by letting them know that it was okay if they, like me, had complicated feelings toward their abusers that included love, and guilt, and pity, and that no one who hadn't experienced abuse could understand. Maybe this book would help them by making them feel less alone, as well as by helping others to understand how complicated the issues really are. And then I thought of all of the girls and young women—like my daughter, Kennedy—who had witnessed some form of abuse growing up, but who were young enough that they still had a chance to heal themselves before reaching the age when they might make the kind of bad choices that would leave them vulnerable and lead them to experience their own abuse. Maybe I could reach them in time to break the cycle of abuse. Maybe I could speak to women with insecurity and self-esteem issues, like I had been plagued with throughout my life, and help them to make better choices than I had.

I had found my mission; to tell my story, and by doing so to explain who Russell really was—even with all of the bad, he was still my daughter's father, and my husband, whom I loved very much. I wanted people to know his good qualities, too, and to understand all that he struggled against in his own tragically short life, which he had ended when he was only forty-seven. And I wanted to explain what our marriage was really like, and hopefully to create something positive out of all of the pain and loss I had experienced. I was going to use this book to answer the question of how I got here, so that hopefully other women would not have to learn the same painful lessons for themselves, and so I could end the cycle of violence—for myself, my daughter, and other women—and let the healing begin.

chapter one

Unworthy of Love

My earliest childhood memory is also my clearest childhood memory. In some ways, it's the only one that really matters because it laid the foundation for who I am and everything that came later in my life.

I was two years old, wearing royal blue zip-up footed pajamas with white plastic feet and a white teddy bear embroidered on the left side. I was sleeping in my parents' bed with my mom when my dad rushed in, yelling, and started punching my mom in the face. Shaking with fear, I jumped up on the bed. I pulled his brown, curly hair, desperately trying to get him to stop beating my mother, who was curled up at the head of the bed, trying to shield herself from his blows.

The carpet was seventies issue brown, and there was a red rotary telephone on a table by the door, but we didn't call for help. We got away from my father and ran out the bedroom's sliding glass door, and then my mom drove to my aunt's house.

My mom has told me that my dad was very jealous, and

that when he was violent it was usually because he had made up a scenario where she had been with someone else. I can remember him yelling at her when I was just a little older. My mom had divorced him by the time I was three.

My mom moved us to an apartment, and from then on, she struggled. She and my father had been high school sweet-hearts, and she was only twenty-one when she had me. Though she was beautiful and thin, with blond hair and blue eyes, and so much going for her, she didn't really date or have much of a social life. She had to work multiple jobs to take care of us, and I'm sure she must have been very lonely. She always seemed to be crying, and I felt guilty from a very young age for being a part of the reason why she was so unhappy. It seemed to me like she had been forced to waste her youth on tak-ing care of me, and that if I hadn't been born, her life would have been better because she could have been out really liv-ing. Obviously, now that I'm a mother myself, I recognize that my mother didn't feel like that at all, but I carried that guilt with me for years.

No matter how hard things were, I knew it was better for us to be away from my father, and I never had a longing to be with him. He remarried quickly and started a new family, and I visited them enough times to see that he hadn't changed. Even now, the vague memories I have of him fill me with dread. He used to always flex his muscles and have me hang from his arm to show me how strong he was. It didn't make me feel safe, like my dad was there to protect me. I felt intimidated, like he was just letting me know what he could do if I made him mad. I also can remember him saying my birth name when he was angry—Shana Lynette Hughes—and I think this association is one of the reasons why I've always hated my name. I never felt like Shana Lynnette Hughes. And because I didn't like who I was, or the life I'd been born into, I always felt like there was someone else I needed to be.

When I was in elementary school, I used to ask my teacher if I could trade names with my friend Melissa for the day, and I would write her name on my papers instead of my own. Melissa was my best friend in first grade, and I wanted nothing more than to be her—a normal kid from a normal American family that had two parents, two cars, a two-story house with a white picket fence, siblings, and a dog. When I went over to her house to play, I always felt different, like I didn't belong there. I didn't want her or my other friends to come over to my house.

Instead of my dream childhood, I had a single mom, and we lived on fish sticks and macaroni and cheese, and I was embarrassed about all of it. I was ashamed that it was just my mom and me, living almost like sisters. Not only that, but we always seemed to be moving, as my mom tried to keep on top of our finances. This transient lifestyle made me feel even more unsettled and insecure. I think this lack of predictability in my early years created much of the anxiety that has plagued me throughout my life.

It was hard for me to go back to school after breaks and hear about my classmates' magical Christmases, with their whole family together at their big, festively decorated houses, and the summer vacations their families had taken from where we lived in Tulsa, Oklahoma to Hawaii or California. We could never afford any of that, and I couldn't be home alone all day while my mom was at work. During my school vacations, I went to stay with my grandparents in Cherryvale, Kansas— Betty White's hometown, which was so small it didn't have a movie theater or a McDonald's, and when my grandfather died a few years ago, we sold his house for less than $10,000.

My grandparents were wonderful people who did so much to help raise me, and I loved spending time with them, but I was also aware of how different this made me from the other kids, and of all I was missing out on. Part of me loved staying with them and never wanted to leave because it was such a simple life, and I could see that for them, it was all they needed to be happy. I think I wished I could be satisfied with that kind of existence, too. But my dreams were already much grander than that. From a young age, I wanted very much to travel and have the kind of big life I felt shut out from at the time. I really looked up to my aunt, who was single and worked in the music industry. She traveled frequently, had beautiful clothes, and lived what seemed to me like an incredibly glamorous life.

To make up for what she couldn't give me as a single parent, my mom overindulged me in other ways. She threw me the most lavish birthday parties we could afford. I've had horrible nightmares my entire life, but especially growing up. My mom let me sleep with her every night. Even in high school, I slept with her most nights, until I went away to college. I know that all of this was her way of loving me, but now that I'm raising a young daughter of my own, I understand that children need structure and consistency to feel safe, and that the lack of either in my early life only added to my problems. The absence of consistent guidelines in our household actually amplified the instability and vulnerability I already felt from the abuse I had witnessed, the ensuing divorce, and my father's absence.

In retrospect, I'm sure there were many other kids in the same situation as I, but I wasn't aware of them at the time. This may have been because this was Oklahoma, which has always been a more traditional state. Back in the seventies, domestic abuse wasn't discussed. There was no outlet or escape, and women and children lived in quiet fear. Divorce was less common, and there were probably fewer single parents there than there were in other, more progressive places. And it wasn't just that I felt different because I didn't have a dad who loved me enough to be a part of my life beyond the $150 a month he paid my mom in child support. I didn't love or value myself, and I felt unworthy of love.

Now that I'm an adult, I've been able to finally forgive my dad and really appreciate how hard my mom worked to provide for me in his absence. I've come to understand the significance of the fact that he was only twenty-one years old when I was born, that they were without resources, that he didn't have the tools to make the marriage work or to be a real father to me. But as a child, all I knew was the trauma of the abuse I had witnessed, and the sorrow caused by not having a dad.

Unfortunately, my mom didn't think to look for these warning signs because the window of abuse had been so small, and I didn't actively miss my father's presence in my life. And of course, I didn't tell my mom what I was really feeling because I didn't want to upset her or make things any harder for her.

I don't know that I could have articulated what I was feeling anyhow. So she had no idea of the crippling insecurities and deficiencies in self-esteem that were consuming my personality and that would haunt me throughout my adult relationships with men and eventually cause me to re-create the domestic abuse I had witnessed in my own life. Even if she had realized that I needed help, we didn't have the means to afford therapy, which wasn't exactly a common practice among the people we knew in Oklahoma at the time anyhow.

By not addressing my significant abandonment issues and low self-esteem, I was prone to trouble with boys from a young age. I needed constant validation from boys, and I began having long-term relationships as early as sixth grade. When my first boyfriend, Kevin, moved away after we had been together for a year, I was so shaken that I considered throwing myself in front of the school bus. The night when he left, I walked around my neighborhood in a pair of socks until there were holes in the bottoms. Of course, first love and its ensuing heartbreak are always particularly intense, but my personal history and psychological scars magnified my grief. It was as though I were being abandoned all over again, and it felt like the biggest loss of my life. And although I have to search my memory to recall this boy's name now, at the time I was convinced my life was over. I was sure that I'd never meet anyone else, and certainly never care about anyone as much as I had cared about him. I didn't want to live without him, but since my life did in fact go on, I had to find another boyfriend.

And so began a lifelong pattern: I always had to have a boyfriend. Without the force of a guy in my life, I became more insecure, nervous, and introverted.

In junior high, my mom moved us to Tennessee so she could take a job in the music industry. We moved back to Tulsa in eighth grade, and my new boyfriend in ninth grade, Jack, was the first boyfriend who made me feel bad about myself.

On Friday nights we often hung out at the high school's football games. Even when Jack and I had made plans to meet, I always felt nervous as I approached him and his friends. I was desperate for any kind of acknowledgment from Jack, but he only looked away while making a joke about me to his friends. He was a cool kid, and that was his way of showing off, but it still hurt. Even though his behavior made me feel horrible about myself, I hung around, hoping for some kind of recognition from him. Instead of getting fed up by his meanness, it only made me want him more. Because I felt worthless, I thought the fact that he treated me as such must make him even more special and desirable. Whenever he pushed me away, I became desperate to do whatever I could to please him.

When pleasing him wasn't enough to make him or any of my later boyfriends stay, I would literally run after them, crying.

"Please, don't leave me," I said, grabbing onto Jack's hand as he tried to shake me off, a disgusted look on his face.

"Please, please, please," I said to boyfriend after boyfriend, again and again, throughout my life.

It's humiliating and painful for me to think back on behavior like this, but it's who I was for years, including throughout my marriage to Russell.

Of course, the problem was that these kinds of relationships only lessened my tenuous feeling of self-worth even more. Because I didn't believe there was anything worth liking about me, I always suspected that the guys stayed only because they felt bad that I was upset, and that they'd just have some new reason to leave next week.

Jack was kind of a wild kid, and I found myself experimenting with alcohol at an earlier age than I probably would have otherwise, because I felt a lot of pressure to be who he needed me to be. He also pressured me into going further than I felt ready for by telling me about a girl we were friends with who had done what he wanted me to do with one of our guy friends. When I still resisted, he teased me.

"If you're too much of a baby, I'll go out with someone else," he said, turning away from me.

As he made a move to get up and leave me, I panicked and gave in. These moments occurred frequently after school because I was a latchkey kid, and some of my friends didn't have parental supervision then, either. Looking back, I feel so lucky that none of us ended up in any kind of trouble. It certainly could have happened.

Even after Jack and I broke up, and I dated several boys in high school who were nicer to me than he had been, I never felt that I could relax and be myself. I always went along with whatever they wanted me to do, including sneaking out of my house at night to join them. I know that in some ways this was just typical high school behavior, but because I didn't have the strength or confidence to stand up for myself, it's fortunate for me that those boyfriends were basically good guys, or else I could have ended up in some bad situations.

Sometimes my insecurity showed up in fairly harmless ways. I had two boyfriends in high school, John and Sam, who were into sports. I instantly volunteered to help out with the teams so I could be around them all the time. Then, when my next high school boyfriend went off to college, I always went up to visit him on the weekends. Supposedly I was staying with my girlfriends who attended the same college, but of course I went straight to his dorm room and stayed with him all weekend. Thankfully, he was also a really nice, respectful guy, because had he not been, I honestly believe I would have gone along with whatever he wanted me to do to maintain the relationship. That's another time I feel lucky that I didn't get myself into more trouble than I did.

At other times my insecurity led me to do things I wasn't proud of then, and I'm even less proud of now. One time, I was on a church ski trip with a large group of kids, one of whom was my friend's boyfriend. My friend wasn't there, and her boyfriend made a pass at me. My boyfriend had just broken up with me. With my self-esteem at an all-time low, getting that attention from this other guy was more important to me than anything else. My need for his approval at that moment was so great that I was unable to honor my friendship by making the decision I knew was right. My girlfriend found out that I had been with her boyfriend behind her back, and it destroyed one of my closest friendships forever.

This was only one of the many ways I sabotaged my friendships when I was growing up. It was scary for me to be emotionally close to people, and I was totally incapable of creating or enforcing any kind of personal boundaries, so I always felt that the girls in my life walked all over me as much as the boys did. Finally, at some point in pretty much every friendship I had, I couldn't take it anymore. I didn't return phone calls; I agreed to go to the movies and then canceled at the last minute. Sometimes this was because I hadn't really wanted to see that particular movie but had been too insecure to speak up. And sometimes it was because I felt so uncomfortable and nervous around other people, because of my constant need to please them, that I preferred being alone to facing the stress of even a friendly social interaction.

I never had the self-esteem to think that people could like me for who I was, and so it always seemed like so much work to keep people happy in the way I felt I needed to in order to maintain friendships. Not to mention that I've always been a total conflict avoider, so anytime a female friend became upset or angry with me, I would avoid the situation rather than talk about it. As I said, with guys I cried and begged them not to be mad and not to leave me. I think I was a disappointment to my friends growing up because I wasn't dependable, and I honestly haven't maintained many long-term friendships.

I couldn't let people get to know me; because I didn't like me, I figured there was no way they could like me, either. As far was I was concerned, I was damaged, imperfect, unlovable. And while I know that these almost sound like textbook descriptions of an abandonment complex, it also occurs to me that they're in the textbooks for a reason.

My whole childhood felt very gray to me. Maybe that's because Oklahoma isn't exactly a bright, sunny place. While it's beautiful in many ways—with its wide-open spaces—it was far from the lush, exotic locales to which I dreamed of escaping. In high school I became obsessed with fashion, and I papered the walls of my bedroom with black-and-white images from fashion magazines, trying to create the glamour I craved, which was in such stark contrast to my surroundings.

Although I adored fashion, I was also stubborn, so when our guidance counselor tested our career compatibility in high school, and my results led them to direct me toward the areas of fashion and photography, I felt offended because this seemed like a stereotypical direction for a girl. I decided to show them just what I was capable of and go in the completely opposite direction. At about this time I had a science teacher who really inspired me, and I decided to turn my focus to science.

Of course, doing things in reaction to other people is never a good idea, and by the time I'd earned my bachelor's degree in biology, and entered a master's program at the University of Oklahoma Health Sciences Center, I realized I didn't know how I had gotten there, or why I had chosen this path. More than that, I also think I had been trying to prove that I could be good enough to be a nurse or doctor and fit into the kind of successful mainstream life I had always felt shut out from as a child. I realized, way too late, that I did want to help people, just not in a clinical setting. But that's how badly I wanted to fit in as a teenager and young adult; I went so far as to choose a career that wasn't right for me just to prove I belonged.

Of course, as a teenager, I didn't have the money to indulge my love of fashion. But my grandparents were generous enough to send me an allowance every month, and I immediately bought the hottest, newest thing that everyone else already had. During my school years, Ralph Lauren Polo was all the rage, and it really was a big deal to wear Polo shirts to school. I had a limited ability to have those, but I did the best I could to keep up and look as good as I could.

Thankfully, I became a cheerleader, which kept me out of a lot of trouble I might have gotten into otherwise. I had cheerleading practice early in the morning. And when we were preparing for the national championships, we practiced again after school until 5:30 p.m., which was closer to when my mom got home from work. And because our squad won a national championship in high school, and then another one in college, that opened doors for me to start traveling and have some of the adventures I had dreamed of for so long.

During the summer, I taught at cheerleading camps run by the National Cheerleading Association, and when we traveled, I found myself gravitating toward the older staff members I met. When I was eighteen, it made me feel safe to date someone who was twenty-two. I didn't understand that it actually made me vulnerable to pressure from guys who were at a different place in their development than I was, and it also further alienated me from people my own age.

Another problem was that as I became busy with my own social life as a teenager, I was keenly aware of my mom's sadness, and I felt guilty about leaving her alone. I could see that she was really struggling and didn't have much of a life of her own, and this was really painful for me. It often felt like she was trying to be my friend because she was young and wanted to have fun, too, but I didn't need another friend. What I really needed, more than anything else, was a mother.

Because I was a cheerleader and on the student council in high school, I think many people saw me as being very confident and secure. But inside I was really struggling. I felt totally out of control emotionally, so I sought to regulate my exterior reality as much as I could. I started controlling my food intake when I was in high school. Partially this was because we had a weigh-in every week during the cheerleading season. But I took my diet way beyond what was reasonable or healthy and struggled with my eating from when I was sixteen to twenty-three.

When I was in college, I used to wet cereal with milk, and then squeeze out all the milk and eat just the cereal. And then I had it down to a science where I could spread out one of those little packages of crackers stuffed with peanut butter to be the only food I ate throughout the day. Finally it got to the point where I tried not to eat at all. On days when we had weigh-ins, I also controlled my liquids because I thought of water as extra weight. I probably had exercise bulimia; I worked out compulsively, twice a day, and for so many hours that I often became injured.

Looking back, I can see what a horrible thing this was to do to myself. It wasn't just about control. My feelings of self-loathing made me hate my body. And my fear of being alone made me worry that if I wasn't physically attractive, I'd never keep a boyfriend. I couldn't believe that guys could like me for any other reason. Because there was obviously nothing good enough about me to love on the inside, I had to make sure I looked good enough on the outside to be desired. Sadly, these were beliefs that would stay with me for a lifetime.

chapter two

Erasing the Girl I Had Once Been

While cheerleading in high school did nothing for my self-esteem or sense of direction, it did open doors when it came time to choosing a college. This was lucky for me, as I didn't have any clear goals, and I seemed to drift wherever chance took me. My main focus and most of my energy were on having and keeping a boyfriend at all times.

I first went away to college at the University of Arkansas, but during my freshman year, my boyfriend was back in Tulsa, so I drove home every chance I could to see him. I guess I felt like I needed to be close to home in some respects, too. Not necessarily to be close to my mom; but because, as much as I felt a desire to travel, I was anxious and self-conscious outside of my limited comfort zone.

Later I transferred to the University of Oklahoma, where I continued studying science. The relationship I had maintained long-distance from Arkansas didn't last, and I ended up dating my cheerleading partner instead. Again, he was older than I, and again, we soon became very serious. We moved in together, and even though I was at an age when many of my classmates were focused on going to parties and exploring life, I was already all about nesting and creating the kind of family life I had always craved. Although I continued to successfully create an illusion of stability and confidence in most areas of my life, I wasn't able to fool everyone. One day, this boyfriend made an observation about me in passing that brought me up short:

"You're going to have a hard time in your life because people see you as so secure, and you're actually so insecure," he said. "They treat you like a secure person, but because you're so insecure, everything is just heartbreaking for you."

At the time I tried to deny his insight, at least internally, but I think it was a pretty astute observation, especially for a nineteen-year-old college student. I'm still working on my insecurity, even today.

Unfortunately, this boyfriend wasn't exactly prince charming, either. He cheated on me and then, when I broke up with him because of this, it took him a while to respect my decision and stop bothering me.

After that relationship ended, I started dating Scott, who also was studying science and who went on to be an orthopedist. He was just as sweet as could be, but we couldn't have been more different. He was very straitlaced and lived the kind of structured life where he measured out his four-ounce chicken breast and vegetables for dinner and washed it all down with a big glass of milk. This was difficult for me to adjust to, coming as I did from such an unstructured household growing up. But as always, I became what I thought Scott wanted me to be and did my best to fit into his life.

The real problems began for me, however, when it was time to meet Scott's physician dad and stay-at-home mom, who had raised him along with his sister and a dog. In other words, he came from exactly the kind of white-picket-fence family that I had wanted so badly as a child.

Instead of feeling like I finally had the opportunity to slip into the life I had always wanted, when I got close to my fantasy, I was terrified. Scott's family could not have been more welcoming or wonderful to me, and yet I did not feel like I fit in. I was sure it was just a matter of time before they discovered I wasn't good enough for their son.

During one of our summer vacations in college, I stayed with Scott and his family at their lake house. The setting was beautiful, and his mother and sister were so kind to me, but I could not relax and enjoy myself. I felt like I always had to be on guard, especially at family dinners. When Scott's sister came back from college, she often reminisced over meals about their wonderful childhood.

I was so conscious of sitting up straight in my chair, with my napkin in my lap, and holding my silverware just so, and smiling, and having the best possible manners. But as Scott's sister began to talk, it was difficult for me to keep my smile in place.

"Do you remember the year we got those bikes at Christmas?" she said, already laughing at what came next.

"Oh, yeah, and we were learning to ride our bikes," Scott joined in.

"And Dad had on that sweater he got for Christmas?" she said.

They all laughed and enjoyed the memory of whatever silly sweater their father had worn that year while I tried to disappear from the table. Obviously, the story itself wasn't the problem. It wasn't like my own childhood had been so terrible by comparison. But most of what I recalled felt transient and more about surviving than enjoying time together as a family. I was already dreading what came next.

"What was Christmas like at your house?" Scott's sister asked me.

I smiled bravely and pushed the food around on my plate with my utensils, thinking of how sad most of my childhood memories seemed.

"Oh, you know," I said.

They all stared at me expectantly, smiling warmly, being the nice people they were. When I didn't elaborate, they started talking about something else. I'm sure they didn't even notice that anything out of the ordinary had happened. But for me, the entire experience was torture. I felt like my stories from my childhood weren't positive, and I didn't want them to know where I had come from, because then they would know that I didn't belong at that table or in that world with them.

At the same time when I was trying—and failing—to feel like I fit into Scott's seemingly perfect family life that summer, I attempted to leave my own troubled childhood behind and become someone else. My mom had married my stepfather, Randall Taylor, who I've called Dad ever since. I wanted to take his last name, so I would share a surname with my family and finally shed all connection with my own father. I found a lawyer in Oklahoma and filed the paperwork to legally change my name to Shana Taylor while I was staying at Scott's family's lake house.

Scott couldn't understand why I felt the need to make this change. I couldn't explain at the time—maybe because I didn't understand it completely—but especially because I was so aware of how different his family life was from mine. I can now see that this was the first step in many I took over the years to try to become my own person by erasing the girl I had once been, and all the shame I associated with her.

It was not long after this, when I was twenty-two, that I also changed my appearance by getting a permanent implant in my upper lip. A few years after that, I got a minor breast augmentation. I didn't like myself, so I kept trying to alter things about my external person. I hoped that by doing so, eventually I would change into someone I liked and therefore finally improve the way I felt on the inside. Of course, at the time I couldn't see that I was just putting Band-Aids on a much deeper problem or that I couldn't keep running away from myself, or my problems, forever.

After I changed my name, my college friends started calling me Taylor. This was a huge relief for me. I finally felt like I'd put some distance between myself and my childhood; as well as from the man who had given me my name and such terrible memories.

Even though Scott could not have been a nicer guy, I spent the nearly five years that we dated fearing I was about to get found out for not being good enough to belong in his world. I felt like there was no way we could ever get married. I thought he needed to marry the girl down the street who had grown up behind a white picket fence, too.

Eventually I sabotaged the relationship. As soon as I lined up another boyfriend, I dropped Scott without ever really giving him an explanation. I knew this was not a nice way to behave toward someone who had always been so kind to me. But I was far too insecure to have an honest conversation about how I was feeling, or even admit that I was seeing someone else. Maybe I was just proving what I'd felt all along, that I wasn't good enough for Scott or the relationship in the first place.

AFTER I LEFT GRADUATE school, with school loans looming, I needed to find a job. With my background in science, pharmaceutical sales seemed like a good fit. I had studied pharmacology, and I knew my way around an operating room. I wasn't able to find a job in Oklahoma or Texas—the two places where I wanted to live at the time—so I relocated to Illinois for an entry-level position.

Again, having a job in sales aggravated my social anxiety, as I probably should have anticipated. There were some mornings when I woke up and could not stand the thought of having to go into a doctor's office or hospital and face people and their questions—and the judgments I felt certain they would level against me.

Although people who knew me had always thought of me as extroverted—the cheerleader and student council leader, and now the sales rep—that perception was completely untrue. Even today, I can only face groups of people if I have time to prepare myself and put on my disguise as a happy, confident person. When people show up unannounced, even friends, or if I have to go into a situation where I'm interacting with strangers in ways I can't control, my anxiety takes over.

I was mostly able to turn on my social side enough to make the sales job work. I didn't really have a choice anyhow, as I needed even the low entry-level salary I was earning because I was suddenly drowning in debt. My mom hadn't had the money to send me to college, so I had substantial student loans. On top of that, I had racked up about $30,000 in credit card debt while I was in college. I was already aspiring to a Beverly Hills lifestyle, even back in Oklahoma, so I had used my credit cards to buy clothes and nice dinners; anything that made me feel sophisticated and worthy. I hadn't understood how quickly it would all add up, or how hefty the interest rates on those college-issued credit cards were. I had hoped that my mom would help me pay this down now that she was remarried. She wisely told me that I had created the problem myself, and I needed to find my own solution. The burden felt insurmountable, but I chipped away at it for years until it was finally paid off. My mom was right about teaching me the lesson; after that, I always used an American Express card that I had to pay off every month. And until very recently, I never again had any substantial debt.

I had dreams of a big life, but I always felt like I was struggling to climb out of the financial hole I had created, and I often wondered how I was ever going to become all that I wanted to be on the salary I was earning. Like many college graduates, I was facing the harsh reality that life was expensive, and it seemed impossible that I'd ever be able to buy a house or even just catch up financially. And I didn't just want to get by. I always thought it was very important for me to earn my own money because I didn't believe anyone would ever want to marry me. My goal was to be like the aunt I'd always admired as a child, and to travel and have that cosmopolitan lifestyle that my mom and I had never experienced.

As much as I tried to make a go of it, I didn't ever love living in Illinois, although I did meet my closest confidant, Dwight, while there, so I'll always be grateful to Illinois for that. I began searching for a job in the more desirable city of Dallas. I finally found a sales position in a different health field and made the jump.

Soon after I moved to Dallas, I attended a conference in another state for work, and while I was there, one of my defining patterns with men resurfaced. At the time, of course, I didn't see it as anything other than an instant and irrevocable attraction.

I was standing in a crowded banquet room at the hotel where the conference was being held when I looked up and locked eyes with a handsome young man across the room. Before I had even spoken to him, I decided that he was the one. I was sure I couldn't be happy without him, and I would do whatever it took to make him mine. Once again, my abandonment issues made it crucial for my self-esteem and sense of self-worth that I gained the approval of this man I had essentially chosen at random, even though I couldn't see how dangerous that was for me at the time.

I had a knack for choosing my men, too. Because I felt so anxious and chaotic inside, I looked for men who appeared to be the most conservative and stable. Without realizing it, by attaching myself to someone who was controlling, I ensured that, at some point, they would control me. And eventually they always did.

Of course, none of this was apparent in my interactions with Chris, and I certainly wasn't aware of my underlying motivations at the time. I thought he was handsome, and I liked his self-confidence. I made eye contact and smiled. I had put so much time and energy into my looks that I felt more confident about my appearance than anything else about my person. So I had the poise to flirt with him, even though I was often shy in other situations. Soon I found a way to join his conversation with several of our other colleagues, and I did everything I could to create a connection. He flirted back, ever so slightly, but did not otherwise encourage my efforts. Of course, my low self-esteem made me see his coolness toward me as a sign of his worth and only made me want him more.

"What are you guys doing later?" I asked, trying to sound light and fun and hide my fear that he might reject me.

I ended up meeting up with Chris and the others for drinks that night and made sure I was in a position to talk with the object of my desire, so we could get to know each other better. There was just one problem. Once we did start sharing details about our lives, I learned that Chris's family owned the company that employed me and that his dad ran the sales department in which I worked.

I had made it obvious that I was interested, but Chris was not.

"This is not going to work," he said.

And yet I relentlessly pursued the situation. The more Chris pushed me away, the more determined I was to make him mine. Just like I had begged my previous boyfriends not to leave me, now that I had decided I needed to have Chris in my life, I had no problem debasing myself to make sure I didn't lose him.

Two days later, he gave in. When the conference ended, I stayed in Florida to be with him. I did go back to Dallas for a month, during which we tried to do the long-distance thing, but we were already far too enmeshed.

I gave up my apartment in Dallas, moved away to be with Chris, and after that we were never really apart again. Because it would have been a conflict of interest for me to date him and report to his dad at work, I quit my job for him and gave up what could have been a very lucrative career. I did not return to work again during our relationship. Not only did I alter these major parts of my life for Chris, my entire personality changed for him as well, even down to the silliest little details. He loved to fish, and so although I've never been outdoorsy, suddenly I loved to fish, too. I was so fearful of losing him that I set out to be whoever he needed me to be, to try to ensure that he would never leave me.

Although Chris's family was very prosperous, that wasn't what drew me to him as the source of the protection I so desperately craved. At the time, he was living in a one-bedroom apartment, and he certainly didn't have a housekeeper or any other trappings of wealth; and yet, the year we spent together while he was living in that apartment was the best of our entire relationship. What made me feel safe was the way the relationship consumed me and my life, taking away any responsibility I might have for making my own decisions or forging my own path. Also, at the time, I felt that being Chris's girlfriend gave me all the self-worth I needed.

Within a year, we were engaged. We moved into a beautiful house and I felt I was on track to having the perfect family I had always dreamed of. We had a good relationship and loved each other very much. He worked hard and we frequently traveled together. I was the stay-at-home woman who did the laundry and made dinner at night. I adored his family and felt like they were becoming my own. But after a while things became strained between us. I was used to working and staying busy, but without any activities or interests outside of our relationship or home, I was going stir-crazy. I was starting to see that the white-picket-fence life didn't fit me for more reasons than I had initially understood. The stable home I had dreamed of seemed mundane and predictable. Maybe we were too young to get married, or maybe I couldn't mold myself to fit this way of life. Either way, I could feel the relationship falling apart, and I was heartbroken.

As much as I tried, it was impossible for me to become the woman Chris needed me to be to fit into his family. Not that I wasn't determined to keep trying. But I think Chris saw more clearly than I did that I was just too free-spirited to be a part of such a traditional clan. Five weeks before our wedding, we called it off, and Chris was definitely the one who chose to end our relationship.

I was devastated when we broke up. Not only was Chris the love of my life, but also I had literally given up everything else to be with him. And I had become anything and everything he wanted me to be. Through no fault of his, I had completely lost myself in the relationship because that was the only way I knew how to have relationships. And so now, without the person who had been defining who I was, I had nothing, not even a clear sense of myself.

I didn't even want to get out of bed in the morning. But I had to do something. So I moved to Fort Lauderdale, Florida, and tried to rediscover the person I had been. But I encountered a problem; that person had never really existed. I had spent my entire life changing myself to fit whatever boyfriend I happened to have at the time, and making most of my life and career decisions in reaction to opinions that people expressed about my personality. Now I was completely on my own, and I had no idea who I was or what I wanted.

In the past, it had been so terrifying for me to be without a boyfriend that I always entered another relationship right away, preferably with a controlling guy who would tell me who to be. But this time I couldn't do that because my heart was broken, and I didn't want anyone but Chris.

For the next few years, Chris and I continued to travel together and see each other sporadically. This probably wasn't that healthy for me emotionally, but what was, in my relationships with men in those days? I didn't want to admit that Chris and I were never going to make it work. And so I wouldn't let go and find someone new, with whom I might actually have formed a lasting relationship. But the lull was good for me because it meant that I went for more than a few months without having a boyfriend for the first time since sixth grade. This time alone allowed me to realize, for the first time ever, that I had a pattern of losing myself in my relationships. I suddenly saw that this wasn't healthy for me and left me with nothing of my own if the relationship fell apart, as all of my relationships eventually did.

During the time when I lived in Fort Lauderdale from 2001 to 2004, I finally spent some time trying to figure out who I was. I returned to a favorite source of escape and self-esteem and began working out twice a day again. I began working in sales and spent most of my time running, reflecting, and trying to recover from my heartbreak.

But I don't know that I was ever completely okay with the fact that I was on my own. And I didn't have the self-awareness to know that I had serious self-esteem deficiencies and abandonment issues and that I needed to do some real work on myself if I was ever going to find the happiness and love I so desperately craved. I didn't ever seek therapy, or even pick up a self-help book, or talk to a friend about the depth of the pain and insecurities that continued to haunt me from my childhood. And so, while I did try to put less weight on having a romantic relationship in my life, I didn't ever really address any of the underlying problems that made me feel the need for a relationship in the first place. It was still hard for me to sleep alone at night, as I continued to be plagued by horrible nightmares. And I didn't ever gain the self-confidence to create a clear vision for my life. Once again, I just sort of drifted.

I didn't want my old name to be a part of my life anymore, so I decided to banish it forever by once again legally changing it. With Taylor as my new first name, I now needed a last name. As I've said, I always loved fashion, and one of my favorite designers has always been Tom Ford. I was a huge admirer of the work he was doing for Gucci at the time, so I decided to take the last name Ford in homage to him.

Finally, I felt like I had shed all connections to my father. Little did I realize that the most important tie—the emotional damage he had done to me—was continuing to haunt me, shaping my personality and my life in disturbing ways that I was completely unable to see. Instead of healing my past and finding a way to love myself, I just kept changing that self. I hoped that eventually I would alter myself enough until I became a person who was unrecognizable from the girl I had been in the past and who I could like.

And then my good friend Tom, who lived in my building, had a stroke. He was paralyzed on one side and was slow to recover his speech. Once again, here was an opportunity for me to completely dedicate my life to someone other than myself. For the next year, I devoted myself to his care and helping to rehabilitate him. I also helped him to run his business, a consumer products e-commerce company. While I'm so glad that I got to help my dear friend, looking back now I can see that it was just like me to take on his goals as my own rather than figuring out what I really wanted to do with my own life. Although I wasn't throwing myself into a romantic relationship, I still felt more comfortable putting someone else before myself and desperately desired the validation of being needed by someone else.

Right around the time when Tom got back on his feet, he was approached by the owner of a family-run textile company. The man wanted to sell his business to Tom so he could retire. The company was based in Los Angeles, and Tom knew that I wanted to relocate to California to be closer to my mom and stepdad, who had moved to Orange County. Because I already had relevant experience, Tom suggested that I take over the company and move to Los Angeles to run it.

In 2004, I moved to a condo in Beverly Hills. I began spending my days running my new textile company from home and going downtown to the warehouse from which my company operated. Although I had made the best of my time alone in Florida, I was still terribly insecure without a boyfriend. It was scary for me to be in a new place without a clear sense of who I should be because, for once, I didn't have anyone there to tell me.

From the outside, it seemed like I had finally achieved the big life I had always dreamed of living. I had literally remade the person I was, with my new lip and breasts. I had renamed myself, shedding all remnants of the name I associated with my father and my unhappy childhood. And I had landed in a totally new reality where I ran my own business, drove a silver Porsche, lived in a beautiful condo in Beverly Hills, and spent my free time at the kind of glamorous locales I had always fantasized about: the Beverly Hills Hotel, the Four Seasons, and the Peninsula.

Of course, none of this was enough to make me feel content or satisfied because, inside, I was still that scared little girl who needed her daddy's approval. Although I was educated and had gained experience in my personal and professional life, I really hadn't matured at all. There was never a moment when I could relax and enjoy my new life or how far I had come. And without having done the work to heal myself, what I thought I needed to finally be happy was a man.

chapter three

Not the Kind of Guy
You Want to Go Out With

When I saw Russell Armstrong from across the room, once again I instantly knew that I had found my man. I was sitting at the bar at the Four Seasons in Beverly Hills, waiting for a friend whom I was meeting for dinner that night.

Russell was with a big group of men with whom he was starting a new company. I already felt drawn to Russell, even though I hadn't spoken to him yet, and one of his friends was talking me up. After chatting with a couple of members of their group, I learned that they were launching a technology company.

The person I was waiting for also was in technology, and so by the time he met me at the bar, we all agreed that my friend and I should join Russell's group for dinner. I had been looking for an opportunity to talk to Russell, so I was thrilled. He was very charismatic, and just the tiniest bit flirtatious, but mostly he remained aloof throughout the meal. What I didn't know at the time was that he had been dealing with a palimony lawsuit from his second son's mother, and she was tall and blond and everything else he thought he saw in me, and so the last thing he wanted was to get involved again.

But, of course, his lack of interest only made me want him more. Even though he hadn't asked for it, I gave him my number at night's end, and I hoped he would call. Instead, he gave my number to one of his friends who had first approached me at the bar.

Russell's friend kept calling me and asking me out, and I'll be honest, it crossed my mind that maybe I should hang out with him so I could get closer to Russell. But I knew that wasn't a very nice thing to do and that it might backfire on me because I was sure Russell would never ask me out if he thought I was dating his friend. It turned out that Russell and I ran in the same circles, so I bumped into him soon after that at one of our usual haunts—the Four Seasons.

When I spotted Russell at the bar that night, I felt so happy to see him and excited that maybe this was my chance to finally win him over. He was pleasant and charming, but again, not overly interested.

"Why haven't you called me?" I asked.

"Give me your number and I'll take you to lunch," he said.

I almost felt like he was only asking me out because I'd made him feel obligated to do so, but I didn't care. I was already so smitten that the more he pushed me away, the more I pursued him.

Again, I gave him my number.

Again, he didn't call me.

At the same time, his friend continued trying to spend time

with me. Finally he called me with an invitation that I considered accepting. Russell's birthday was December 21 and his group of friends had planned a surprise party for him that year, and Russell's friend asked me to attend. I very much wanted to attend, so I could see Russell. I bought a very nice bottle of wine to take to the party, and then I sat on my couch, twisting the bottle in my hands, thinking.

Do I go?

I really wanted to see Russell. But I was afraid that if I went with his friend, Russell would think I was dating his friend.

Do I not go?

I really wanted to see Russell.

Do I go?

And then an even worse thought occurred to me: if I went to the party and Russell was there with another woman, I knew it would break my heart. Finally I opened the bottle, drank the wine, and stayed home. More than anything else, I was afraid that Russell's opinion of me might change if I showed up with his friend, who had a reputation for dating every woman in town. I didn't want Russell to think that I was the kind of woman who would go out with a guy like that.

Later that week, Russell's persistent friend invited me to a Christmas party with a proposition that finally wore down my resistance.

"Listen, I know that you don't want to go out," he said. "But just go with me. There's going to be a lot of people there, and you're new in town, so you can meet some new people."

It was true that I still didn't know many people, so I agreed. I met him at the Beverly Hills Hotel and rode with him to the party. Only, when we got there it was mostly older guys with money and young, half-dressed women looking for their next sugar daddy. The whole setup felt very sleazy and not the kind of thing I wanted to be around. I called a cab and left.

As I later learned, Russell saw his friend at the office the next day.

"How was your date?" Russell asked.

"She left," his friend said. "She disappeared."

Russell knew exactly what kind of party his friend had invited me to and, apparently, hearing that I hadn't been interested in being with that crowd made him think that maybe I wasn't the type of girl he'd originally thought, and that maybe he should ask me out after all. Of course, I later learned that Russell had good reason for wanting to avoid ending up with a woman who wanted him only for his money, but I didn't know any of this at the time. All I knew was that when we next ran into each other, he engaged with me in a way he hadn't before.

As we sat at the bar, he appraised me over his drink.

I gave him a flirtatious smile, hoping this would be the night he finally asked me out. But when he spoke, it wasn't to proposition me.

"You're a nice girl," he said. "I'm not the kind of guy you want to go out with."

"Yes, you are," I said, laughing and trying to keep the tone light.

"I'm not an easy guy," he said.

He went on to tell me that he had two sons with two different exes, and to warn me, repeatedly, that I shouldn't get mixed up with him. Of course, I should have been a better listener because he was trying to tell me exactly who he was and where he was at in his life. But I took his candor as a sign that he was honest and responsible and therefore just the kind of guy I wanted to date. Once I had made up my mind to be with a person, as I had done with Russell and most of my exes before him, I wanted to believe that they were perfect, so I dismissed any information that might suggest otherwise.

It got to the point that winter when every time I met my friend Jennifer for drinks, I hoped I would run into Russell. After we finally got together, Russell always liked to tell people that I chased him for three months. It wasn't quite that bad, but I definitely had a crush on him. Finally, in early February, we ran into each other again and made a date to go out to dinner. He texted me to finalize our plans later that week, and then took me out for the first time on Valentine's Day.

I was so nervous as I got ready for our date that night. After much indecision, I finally decided to wear a gray dress that I thought looked cute without seeming like I was trying too hard. When Russell arrived at my house to pick me up, he seemed pleased with my appearance.

"Wow, you look beautiful," he said.

That was always his line, and it made me feel amazing every time he said it.

I beamed at him, so excited to finally be going out with this guy I'd liked so much for so long. He handed me a small box, and when I opened it, there was a beautiful Franck Muller watch inside.

As always, Russell was the picture of poise and success, from his impeccable suit to the silver Mercedes in which he whisked us off to dinner. Our conversation was effortless. He seemed so incredibly charming and mature, so strong and confident. As Craig David crooned on the CD player, Russell reached over and held my hand, releasing a million butterflies inside me. For years after that night, we frequently listened to that Craig David CD, and each time we did, it reminded me of the absolutely best days at the beginning, and the intense feelings I had for him from the start. Although it is too painful for me to listen to that CD now, I know that if I did, it would unleash just as many romantic feelings, and maybe a few butterflies, too.

"I hope you like Italian," he said.

"Love it," I said. "Where are we going?"

"Dolce," he said.

"Oh, of all the places for us to go," I said.

He looked over and gave me a questioning look. I often went to Dolce and had recently gone on a date with a man who also frequented the restaurant. Nervous that I might be about to step into an awkward situation, I figured it was best to be honest.

"Someone that I've gone out with goes there all the time," I said.

It wasn't like I was dating the guy seriously, or anything like that, but I didn't want to hurt his feelings by having him see me there with another man on Valentine's Day.

Russell didn't have much of a response, so I figured it wasn't that big a deal to him, and just hoped the guy wouldn't be at the restaurant that night. When we walked in, I was relieved to see that he wasn't there. Only, as my date with Russell progressed, I discovered that the situation was far from okay. When the waiter left us alone after delivering our food, Russell started in on me.

"Well, I didn't know you were fucking the bartender here," he said.

I looked up at him in surprise. I couldn't believe he had spoken to me like that on our first date, and he sounded genuinely angry. But because I had decided that Russell was perfect from the first moment I saw him, I quickly made excuses for his behavior, and continued to see him in his idealized form. As I had long been conditioned to do, I immediately set to work trying to calm him down and win him over to my side.

"He's not the bartender," I said. "He's friends with the owners, so he hangs out here a lot, and he knows the bartenders and waiters."

"Oh, I didn't know you were into bartenders," Russell said.

"Actually, he's in finance," I said.

But Russell continued to degrade the person I had been out with until finally I was staring at my plate of ravioli with tears in my eyes, trying not to let on to everyone else in the restaurant that the man I had been so excited to go out with had made me cry.

As usual, I assumed that if someone was angry, it was my fault, especially because I already thought so highly of Russell and his intelligence and poise. Rather than standing up to Russell, I attempted to calm him down.

"I'm so sorry," I said. "I just wanted you to know in case we ran into the guy."

Russell apologized and explained that other women had

burned him in the past. I let him know that I understood how this could make him suspicious and reassured him that I was happy to move on with what had otherwise been a wonderful night. And I was. From the first moment I saw Russell, I always thought of him as the handsome, charismatic, successful man I had instantly fallen for, no matter what he did. Soon he was his usual charming self again, talking about the fast-paced world of venture capital in which he worked, and showing himself to be an excellent storyteller who often made me laugh. By evening's end, when he dropped me home and kissed me good night, I was convinced he was the best date ever, and I could hardly wait for our next night out.

When I woke up the next morning, a whirlwind of texts began flying back and forth between us. We would text each other all day, every day, and he was always sending me messages that read things like "I'm sitting in a boardroom of attorneys and all I can think about is you." As I read Russell's sweet words, I was overjoyed about how romantic he could be. Before I knew it, I was falling in love.

It was all happening just like I had hoped it would. I said something about this to Russell on one of our next dates.

"I told you we're going to be together," I said. "Here you were blowing me off all this time. But I knew."

Just like with my previous relationships, we were never really apart after that, except for occasionally when he had to travel for business. Russell loved business more than anything else, and from the moment he woke up in the morning until he went to bed, he was constantly on his BlackBerry.

I quickly began spending time with Russell and his many

business associates and potential clients, and I immediately loved the lifestyle. Our social calendar was always full, and we went out to dinner almost every night. Russell was the ringleader, and he always brought along new and interesting people. He was spontaneous, which made our new life together so much fun. On many nights, after having dinner with a big group of business associates, we would check into a hotel for a romantic stay, and he would go into work late the next morning, just so he could spend more time with me. Considering how much he loved and valued his work, this gesture meant a great deal to me.

I was totally crazy about Russell, and he loved to brag about our relationship.

"She's craaaaazy about me," Russell often said to our friends.

And he was right.

I had fallen quickly, and so had he. And the feelings I had for Russell were far deeper and more passionate than anything else I had ever experienced.

Of course, as I'd always done, I withdrew from all other areas of my life to put all my energy into Russell and our relationship. Before Russell and I began dating, I had spent most of my free time with my friend Jennifer. She expressed to me that she was starting to feel frustrated with me because I was always with Russell now.

The first or second weekend after Russell and I started dating, I finally made plans to hang out with Jennifer. Several guys from Russell's office were going out that night, and Jennifer was friendly with one of the guys. He asked her to join them, and she asked me to join her. Russell had his sons for the weekend, so he couldn't go along.

Russell had told me that he really wanted me to meet his children, which of course was a big deal because I took it as a sign that he was as serious about our relationship as I was. I honestly would have preferred to spend the night with Russell, but I was trying to be a better friend than I had been in the past. And Russell knew it was important for me to respect my friendship, so he suggested that I go out with Jennifer on Friday night and then come down to his house in Manhattan Beach on Saturday night so I could meet his sons and spend the rest of the weekend with them. I was looking forward to being with Russell and his kids and seeing what it would be like to be a permanent part of his life.

On Friday night, Jennifer and I met up with her friend at the Chateau Marmont. When we joined him at a table in the hotel's garden, he was with two friends, including an athlete from out of town with whom he was doing business. The five of us had drinks and dinner, and then we all went dancing at the Spider Room in Hollywood.

It was nice to see Jennifer and I was having fun, but I kept missing Russell, imagining him at his house with his boys. We texted each other frequently throughout the night; he was trying to be supportive, and I was telling him that I was looking forward to seeing him the next day. Everything seemed really good between us, and I couldn't wait for our reunion. At the end of the night, I left the club with Jennifer and went home to get a good night's sleep for the day ahead.

When I woke up on Saturday morning, all I could think

about was getting to see Russell later that day. Only, when I called him to make plans for when I should arrive at his house, he didn't answer. When I texted him, he didn't respond. At first I figured he was just busy with the boys. But then, after an hour, when I still hadn't heard from him, all my old insecurities started to surface, and I began texting him and texting him, desperate for a response. Finally he wrote back:

"I'm just going to spend the weekend with my kids."

I had no idea what had happened to change his mind, and I texted him back right away. No reply. I went into my old mode of wanting to do anything to get him to stay with me, and I kept texting and calling. Nothing.

I was confused and upset and tried to calm myself down by taking a bath, but nothing worked. He had cut me off completely, and no matter how often I replayed all of our communication from the night before, and the last few times we had seen each other, I couldn't think of why.

I didn't hear from Russell for a couple of days, during which time I was a total mess. I couldn't focus on work, or friends, or anything else but him, and wondering what I had done wrong to derail our romance.

We were in such a new relationship that this obviously should have been a warning sign for me, but all I wanted was to find a way to patch things up and get back together with him. I was an especially big mess because I knew that getting to meet his kids was a really big step, and I had been thinking that we'd get to play house that weekend. Instead, he had shut me out completely without explanation.

Finally, I called Russell once again, and he picked up. I was relieved, but also nervous.

"You hooked up with that athlete the other night," he said.

"What?" I said, totally shocked. "What are you talking about?"

But he was adamant about it.

"Yeah, the next day, my friend called me and told me that you hooked up with that athlete," he said.

"But I didn't," I said. "I went home with Jennifer. That's ridiculous. I don't want to be with anyone but you, Russell."

I couldn't understand how Russell could make something like that up and be so sure about something I hadn't done. But however it had happened, it was clear that in his mind the story was true, and there was no way he was going to give me a chance to defend myself or explain. I tried again and again to convince him that nothing had happened, but I could tell he didn't believe me.

Before any of this happened, Russell and I had made plans to attend a charity event together, so we agreed that we would still go. When we met up at the Four Seasons that night, I was so happy to see him and relieved that he seemed to have forgiven me. He wasn't particularly warm to me, but even when our relationship was going well, he was never a publicly affectionate person. I tried to convince myself that everything would be fine once we had spent some time together and he could see how much I cared about him and remember how much fun we had together.

After the event, we ended up back at the Four Seasons,

where I had left my car. We were out with a big group of Russell's business associates, and we were all sitting in the bar near the piano at two tables that had been pushed together. Russell had had a few drinks over the course of the night, and I could see that his mood had shifted. He leaned over to me so the others couldn't hear.

"I know that you fucked that athlete," he hissed.

"What are you talking about?" I said, embarrassed and upset as I looked around to see if anyone else had heard what he said.

"You're just like everybody else in this town," he said.

"Russell, please," I said.

Everything in my neat little fantasy of my romance with Russell was melting down, and I could barely keep my composure. If he had asked me to, I probably would have dropped to the floor with him, or done anything he asked in that moment.

We couldn't really talk with so many people around, and I was hoping that we could leave soon so I could try to understand where his accusations were coming from and how to make them stop.

Russell got up from the table without saying anything else.

After ten minutes had gone by and he still hadn't returned, I realized that he hadn't gone to the bathroom or stepped outside to make a phone call. He had left me there alone with his business associates.

I started texting and calling him, but he wouldn't answer.

I ran outside, retrieved my car from the valet, and started racing toward his house in Manhattan Beach. Eventually I saw his silver Mercedes in front of me and caught up to him. When he recognized my Porsche, he finally answered my call. I tried to calm him down.

"Russell, please, I didn't do anything with him or anyone else," I said.

"Fuck you," he said.

"I went home with Jennifer," I said.

"You're a whore," he said.

"I don't want to be with anyone but you," I said.

"I don't ever want to see you again," he said. "Get the fuck out of my life. I don't want to have anything to do with you."

"Russell, please, please don't do this," I said.

"I don't want this," he said. "I don't want a relationship."

"I'm so sorry," I said. "Please don't be mad at me."

"Just get out of my life."

He hung up on me. I was crying hysterically as I called Dwight and told him the story through tears.

"He left me," I said.

"What do you mean, he left you?" Dwight asked.

"He got mad at me and left me at the Four Seasons," I said. "I'm following him to Manhattan Beach now so we can talk about it."

"That's ridiculous," he said. "Why are you bothering to follow him? He's obviously an asshole."

But I had made up my mind that Russell was the one, just like the other men from my past who I had chosen right away because they instantly made me feel safe, and there was no convincing me otherwise. I followed him to his house and pulled into his driveway right behind him. When we got inside, he screamed and screamed at me. He kept trying to get away from me, and I kept following him, crying, and begging him to listen to me. We ended up in one of the upstairs bedrooms, and he continued his outburst, but no matter what I said, he had made up his mind that I had had sex with this athlete and he kept telling me that it was over.

Finally he went into one of the other bedrooms to go to sleep. I was so worked up that I knew I wouldn't be able to fall asleep. But I didn't want to leave, so I took a bath, as I always do when I'm upset. Russell came in while I was in the tub. I did my best to smile at him but he only scowled at me in return.

"You're so skinny," he said. "It's disgusting. You're like a skeleton. It's not sexy."

I felt so vulnerable, being naked in front of him while he criticized me so venomously, but I didn't want to stand up and reveal myself even further. At last, he went back to bed, and I sat and cried in the tub.

Of course, I should have left his house that night and never looked back, but I was hooked on the roller-coaster ride of the relationship, and the need it brought out in me to please him. He seemed to be hooked, too. Instead of breaking up, we established a pattern: he flew into a rage over the smallest thing, or sometimes over nothing more than a figment of his imagination. I apologized, and cried, and begged and pleaded, and vowed to myself that I would find a way to be so perfect that he'd never get angry again. From the beginning, I began compiling a careful mental inventory of all of the many things I needed to avoid doing or saying to keep the peace in our relationship.

Top on this list was the fact that Russell had to reach me immediately, at all times, or else he would fly into a rage. Sometimes even being careful not to be unavailable wasn't enough, though.

When we first started dating, I was getting ready to have a facial in Beverly Hills one day. I was at a spa, in my robe, and they had put this electrical mask on my face to stimulate my skin before the treatment. My cell phone started ringing, but I couldn't answer it because I was already in the room with the aesthetician. And with that mask on, I wasn't even able to see my phone. When she finally removed the mask, and I saw that I had missed a call from Russell, I was panic-stricken. I knew he would be furious that he hadn't been able to reach me, and that it had now taken me fifteen minutes to return his call. I told the woman I'd be right back, stepped outside into the hallway, still in my towel, and called him.

"What are you doing?" he asked.

"Nothing," I said. "What are you doing?"

"I know you're not doing nothing because I've been trying to reach you for fifteen minutes," he said. "You're obviously with someone."

I knew where this was going and my heart started pounding.

"No, I'm in the middle of getting a facial," I said.

"You're a fucking liar," he said.

"No, I swear to you," I said.

"I know you're with someone," he said

"I'm at the Face Place," I said. "Call the front desk and check. I have an appointment. Just call the number."

"Fuck you," he said. "Get the fuck out of my life."

He hung up on me. By this point, I was hysterical. I went back into the spa and told them that I needed to leave immediately. Not that it did any good. I called Russell all day long, maybe twenty times, but, of course, he wouldn't take any of my calls. We had plans for that night, and when I met up with him at the restaurant where we were dining, he lit into me.

"If you ever lie to me again about what you're doing, that's it," he said.

"I didn't lie. I said, 'Nothing, what are you doing?' Because that's what people say," I said.

"You're a fucking liar," he said. "If you ever don't tell me exactly what you're doing again, that's it."

Again, instead of questioning the complete irrationality of what he was saying, and the unbelievable rage it had inspired in him, I started to believe that he was right, and that maybe it was my fault he was mad because I hadn't known to tell him *exactly* what I was doing.

"I'm sorry," I said. "It won't happen again."

I immediately set out to change my behavior so that nothing like this would *ever* happen again. But the problem was that no matter how diligently I followed Russell's every command—down to how I should dress, and how I should behave when I interacted with my friends—he kept changing the rules, and he never gave me warning of this until it was too late.

When he got mad, his default reaction was to tell me to get out of his life, which triggered my deepest fears of abandonment and made me even more determined to make him stay.

Even so, I never could relax and feel like we were going to be together forever, because I always felt like, at any moment, he was going to end our relationship.

Confusingly, at the same time, I made the greatest memories of my life with Russell. We traveled together, went out together, and spent hours talking about what we wanted from our futures. He was seven and a half years older than I, and his maturity and experience allowed him to be like the father I'd always wanted. He had a successful business and real responsibilities, including children, and the stability of his life was comforting to me. He told me countless stories about his business ventures and all of the interesting projects on which he had worked. He had more life and business experience than I did, and he gave me advice about so many things. He was the leader, and I was content to follow. In fact, I preferred to follow, because it made me feel safe.

From the beginning, Russell made it clear that he was in charge of things. One of his favorite phrases was, "I'm driving this bus. If you think this is a relationship of equality, you're wrong. This is not a fifty-fifty deal." He always said this in a slightly sarcastic tone, and I laughed when he did, but I knew he was sincere. And I was fine with that. He was strong and independent, and I respected him and trusted his lead.

Russell also maintained his control over me by monitoring my phone. When I wasn't looking, he used to take my phone out into his garage and scour my call log and text messages for any reason to be suspicious of me. When we were first dating, all it took to set him off was the fact that I had the name of an infamous NBA player in my phone book. I had never once called the guy. I hadn't received any calls from him since before I'd met Russell. There wasn't any evidence of contact between us in my call log. But Russell was instantly jealous.

The story of how I'd gotten the guy's number was funny, so I tried to explain. Back when I'd been living in Fort Lauderdale, years before I'd even met Russell, I was out at a restaurant when this player from the Miami Heat saw me talking to the maître d', whom I knew. He asked the maître d' for my number and called me.

"I have a wife, and I have a black girlfriend, but I don't have a white girlfriend right now," he said. "And I always have a black girlfriend *and* a white girlfriend."

It was all I could do not to laugh out loud.

This is your pickup line? I thought. *You have a vacancy you'd like me to fill.*

"You're hysterical," I said. "And although I am sure I should be flattered, you've got the wrong girl."

That was pretty much the extent of it. He did call me a couple times, even after I had moved to Los Angeles, and invite me out to a game when his team played the Lakers. I never went, and I was never even tempted. But, of course, I was flattered. And being a girl from Oklahoma, I thought it was kind of cool that I had this famous basketball player's cell phone number. It wasn't like I was going to call him, but it was a funny story, and kind of a novelty to have him in my phone. Russell wasn't amused.

"You fucked him," he said.

"No, I didn't," I said.

"He used to take care of you," he said.

"What are you talking about?" I said. "I never even went out with him."

"He bought a condo for you that you lived in," he said.

As the story became increasingly elaborate, Russell became even more furious. There was nothing I could do to convince him that his fantasy wasn't true, down to the tiniest fabricated details. And for years after that, every time we had a fight, he would bring up the story of my NBA sugar daddy. This used to drive me completely crazy because it was one thing to get in trouble for things I'd actually done, but to be screamed at for something that was totally fabricated really bothered me. Not that I ever dared to even open my mouth about any of this around Russell, of course.

chapter four

The Cost of Protection

There were red flags all over the place, even when Russell and I were first dating, that the relationship was unhealthy. It's embarrassing for me to look back now because it really speaks to my own lack of self-worth and abandonment issues that I would still get involved with someone when part of me could see the problems from the beginning. But, of course, at the time I was still totally dominated by my insecurities and the intense emotions I had for Russell. I didn't heed any of the warning signs because I was too busy making sure, at any cost, that I didn't lose my relationship with him. And so I didn't realize he had already begun the grooming process by which abusers prime the people they hurt to take even more. I don't think he had any idea it was happening, either; it was a collision of unconscious insecurities—his and mine—that created our relationship, just as happens with all codependent relationships.

Russell had such a quick temper that I often had no idea

what had set him off. It could be something as simple as if I had one of my girlfriends at the table with me when we were out for dinner, and I spent too much time talking to her. Or if he felt like I was too talkative with one of his business associates.

If I gave Russell too much attention, I was being needy. But he didn't like it when I didn't give him enough attention, either, because he said it made him feel disrespected. Instead of speaking to me about this in the moment, Russell would just get up and leave me wherever we were, like he had done that night at the Four Seasons. He left me several times at restaurants and parties, usually with his business associates, none of whom I knew that well. At times when I didn't have my own car with me, I had to sheepishly ask someone else to give me a ride home, which was totally embarrassing, or take a cab. One time, Russell left me on Laurel Canyon Drive late at night. As I huddled alone in the dark on the side of the street, dressed in a black sheath, I frantically called my mom, and then Dwight, and then my mom, and then Dwight, trying to get someone to answer and pick me up. I reached my mom, who was visiting us at the time. Russell had gone home after abandoning me and told my mom that I had stayed behind to be with friends who were driving me home. This was a total lie, told right to my mother's face; the event was for business, and I didn't have a single friend there. Once my mom heard the truth, she didn't say a word. She frantically jumped in her car and raced to find me. As she drove, I'm sure she had nightmare visions of all of the dangers that could befall me. When she pulled up alongside where I stood, and I got in the car with her, we were both really worked up. We didn't talk about what had happened much on the ride home. I was embarrassed that she had witnessed how little respect the man I loved had for me. I was dreading what would happen when I saw Russell at home and thinking about how I could calm his anger. It turned out that Russell had left me because he thought I had been too impressed by a magician who had been entertaining guests with card tricks at the event. Russell claimed that I had once again embarrassed him with my dumb-blonde behavior.

I wasn't the only one that Russell got mad at. He had more conflict in his life than anyone else I'd ever met. He had two kids with two different women, one of whom had sued him for palimony. It wasn't uncommon for him to end a business phone call by screaming into the phone and hanging up on the other person. He wrote venomous e-mails to people when he wasn't getting his way. I excused these behaviors because he was a serious businessman and a tough negotiator, and I thought this was his way of winning.

But some incidents were hard to justify. I once met a man, Brian, when I was out with Russell in Beverly Hills. Together, the two men told me the story of a fight they had gotten into years before. At the time, Brian was Russell's neighbor in Beverly Hills and had invited Russell over for a party. During the course of the night, Russell felt Brian had disrespected him in front of the other guests. Russell left the party, only to return after the festivities had ended. When Brian opened the door, he found Russell waiting for him.

"I am going to kick your ass," Russell said. "Do you want me to do it in your house or outside?"

Leave it to Russell to be a gentleman right before he kicked your ass.

They walked into the kitchen and fell to blows.

At this point in the story, Russell interjected that he was concerned about the number of knives in the kitchen; he didn't specify whether he was worried that Brian would grab a weapon and escalate the fight, or that he would.

But Russell managed to use his blows to drive Brian outside, where the altercation continued. According to both men, Russell then dragged Brian into his own swimming pool and held him under until he stopped fighting back. Only then did Russell apparently feel like he had proven that he was worthy of Brian's respect and consider the fight over, at which point he pulled Brian out of the pool.

Brian laughed as he recounted this story to me.

"Your husband almost killed me," Brian said.

I couldn't believe what I was hearing. It didn't seem like a laughing matter to me.

I didn't know about this last incident until much later in our relationship. But the rest of the conflict was evident everywhere in Russell's life. By nature I'm a conflict avoider, and so by choosing to be with Russell, it's almost like I threw myself into the lion's den; maybe I was looking for a lion to protect me because I didn't feel capable.

With all of my insecurities and vulnerabilities, I should have gone for some sweet guy who doted on me, but just like with all of my other relationships, I didn't think I deserved someone who treated me well. And what I felt I needed, more than kindness, was someone strong who could protect me from the unpredictable world around me. The fact that Russell was the controlling type made the whole relationship even more appealing—even if not consciously—because it meant that I could throw myself into pleasing him instead of figuring out what I wanted.

I also felt a huge sense of relief when Russell started opening up to me about his own childhood, which was much worse than anything I had ever experienced. After feeling like I had needed to hide my true self and my past from all of my former boyfriends with their white-picket-fence families, I had finally found a man who didn't make me feel like I had an inferior upbringing. Instead, in a way, I felt like I was home.

Russell had grown up in government-sponsored housing in a neighborhood in the southwestern area of Dallas called Oak Cliff, which he often compared to South-Central LA or Compton. He told me that he had been in countless street fights as a kid while trying to defend himself. He shared that his father used to take him to bars, sit him on a bar stool, order him a Shirley Temple, and they'd hang out for a while. According to Russell, his parents had a volatile relationship, which wasn't hidden from him. He also said that when he was eight years old he watched one of his best friends be shot and killed by a security guard when his friend walked into a convenience store with a stick in his hand, and the guard thought it was a weapon.

When Russell told me all of this, I felt horrible for him. Here was this man I loved who had been through so much at such a young age. I knew that he was an adult and still needed to be responsible for his actions toward me, but I also wanted to mother him and make up for all that he had lost in the past. I now understood his anger and the difficulty he had in trusting people; especially those he loved. I wanted, more than ever, to hold him and tell him that I would be there for him, and love him, no matter what. I could see that Russell needed love, and although he was resistant to letting his guard down, I believed that if I could just get through to him, I could change him. I could take away the fear that drove him to anger. I could be the one to help him get over his childhood pain and trust again.

I felt closer to him, like I had met my match and could finally let my guard down about my own struggles. I told Russell about my own childhood experiences, and while I didn't have the self-awareness at the time to talk about the insecurity it had inspired in me, it was a relief to finally share. We definitely bonded over our childhood challenges and how far we had come. We were like this amazing team, and it felt so good to be that close with a man who I was falling in love with.

Also, I have to admit that the scared little girl inside of me felt safe being with a man who told me he had fought Golden Gloves and would brag about beating people up. Russell made it clear that he would do anything to keep me safe. And even if the cost of protection was that he also turned his aggressive personality on me, as far as I was concerned, having that shield around me made everything else worthwhile.

Not only was I predisposed to make excuses for even Russell's worst behavior, but there was a great deal that attracted me to him as well. He was a natural storyteller and a born salesman. He could be very good company. This may sound strange, but a good compatibility test for me was to find someone I could run errands with and still have fun. Russell was that guy for me. He had three thousand people in his phone, and he led a spontaneous, action-packed lifestyle. This was not only attractive to me because it was the kind of life I had always craved, but it was also the exact opposite of the traditional home life I had not felt good enough to maintain with my former fiancé.

Here, finally, was the kind of unstructured life that was comfortable to me because I had grown up with so few boundaries and rules. I've always felt anxious even just thinking about having a standard job where I would have to sit at a desk from nine to five. This was the exact opposite of that kind of routine, and I liked it.

All of this was very seductive to me, and I quickly became hooked on the chaos and unpredictability. Looking back, I think that it was just one more distraction from being responsible for my own decisions or life, or the need to look at my issues or grow as a person. I've never liked to sit still, because that's when I'm forced to reflect, and always end up feeling stressed out, so the constant action felt like the perfect fit for me.

And while having to respond to a constant stream of new people and situations had overwhelmed me when I was younger, this was different because I now experienced everything through the filter of Russell and my focus on being exactly who he needed me to be. As always, his control over me felt very reassuring and safe.

Because of the type of business Russell was in, and the type of personality he had, Russell was forever getting involved in new ventures, so there were plentiful new people to meet and new deals to close—from a Koo Koo Roo Chicken franchise, to a nightclub, to a technology company. It was really interesting to watch all of these different types of deals go down.

Our life together was exciting and fun. Russell was always the instigating force and the consummate host. He was the first one to reach for the check, and since these dinners cost $1,500 to $2,000, I assumed his business was doing very well. This was also attractive to me, not because being with a rich man was my end goal—it was much more his physical strength that made me feel safe—but it certainly felt good to be with a successful man who could take care of me.

Russell would suddenly take me with him to Miami one weekend. And then, the next weekend, we'd be heading to Las Vegas. I had once traveled to conventions with my ex-fiancé, but I hadn't had that in my life for a while. I realized I had missed the action, and I enjoyed the pace of my new life.

"You are a professional vacationer," Russell used to say to me. "You love to be gone, and traveling, and on the move."

It was true. I've always called this the "geographical cure"— the more you move around, the less time you have to be still and quiet with yourself. Such time for reflection could have allowed me to become self-actualized, something I was far from ready for.

Some of the best times Russell and I had together were when we were traveling. Early on, we went to Miami to look into purchasing a nightclub business. The whole trip was so

much fun; lots of big, festive dinners with his business associates, and nights spent dancing and hanging out at nightclubs.
One night when I was cold, Russell bought me a beautiful,
cream-colored silk Dolce & Gabbana wrap. That was just the
kind of gesture he often made that caused me to feel like he
cared about me.

But one night, when we were at the club, after Russell had
had a few drinks, his mood changed once again. By this point
I knew the warning signs immediately. His drink was Crown
Royale and Coke, and he had given me good reason to say to
him, "Whiskey makes you mean."

On this night in Miami, Russell leaned over to me so the
rest of our group couldn't hear him.

"It's so embarrassing, the way you laugh all the time," he
said.

"I'm sorry," I said, instantly looking for a way to talk him
down.

By the time we got back to our hotel and started getting
ready for bed, it was clear that there was more going on with
Russell than I'd first realized, and calming him down wasn't
going to be so easy.

Not that I didn't try.

"You have scars all over your back from having sex in the
Beverly Hills Hotel and the Four Seasons!" he screamed at me.

"I never even spent the night at the Beverly Hills Hotel or
the Four Seasons in LA," I said. "And I don't think I have scars
on my back."

But he wasn't listening to anything I said. He was furious.

"You're a whore," he said. "You fucked all these guys in the

Four Seasons and the Beverly Hills Hotel, and now you've got scars all over your back to prove it."

This went on for at least an hour. He raged and screamed at me and kept grabbing my arms to get my attention, and he wouldn't listen to a word I said in my defense, no matter how much I cried and pleaded. Russell was so convinced of his story that by the end of the night I started to question myself. Maybe I did have scars on my back. Not from having sex, obviously, but possibly I'd gotten them when I was a kid, and I'd just never noticed them because I'd never really looked. By the end of the night, I was sitting on the bathroom counter, holding my shirt up, looking for scars on my own back.

"Well, if there are scars, it could have been from gymnastics when I was little," I said, twisting my neck to get a better view.

As I looked in the mirror, I caught sight of Russell's reflection: His eyes had changed. It was almost like he wasn't even looking at me anymore; he had this fixed stare on his face—his eyes didn't seem to move or blink at all. It was as if he were gazing right through the mirror. Or he had been so completely swallowed up by his rage that none of his other personality traits, or any other human emotions, were left inside him beyond his anger, and he wasn't there anymore.

That was one of the first times I ever saw that look on Russell's face, and it unsettled me because it was like he wasn't really there in the room with me anymore. That, paired with the fact that he was so adamant about the scars and truly seemed to believe that they were visible on my back and had concocted a whole story to explain how they had gotten there, made me have a disturbing thought: *What if he's having para-noid delusions and he sees scars where there are none?*

That night really scared me, because I truly began to won-der if Russell had some sort of a mental illness, like a form of schizophrenia, where he was hearing voices that were giving him information. I knew that Russell's mother struggled with mental illness. When Russell and I had first started dating, his mother was exhibiting severe symptoms of her hypomania—erratically buying a Jaguar she couldn't afford, driving the wrong way on the interstate—and she was in the process of being institutionalized. Russell was always having to take phone calls from his family to help them handle the responsi-bility of his mother's care.

I found myself worrying for the first time that maybe men-tal illness ran in Russell's family. At least the other times he had gotten mad, his anger had had some basis in reality. It really had taken me fifteen minutes to call him back that day of my facial. I really did have an NBA player's number in my phone. But this reason for his outburst was completely fabri-cated from thin air. And even more frightening, he had almost been able to convince me that his dark fantasies were true, even though they were about my own body.

By the end of the night, as usual, I reverted to my insecu-rities. I was crying hysterically and pleading with him not to be mad.

After a few hours I was finally able to calm Russell down enough for us to go to bed, but I couldn't sleep, and I lay awake hoping that everything would be better in the morning. But the next day, he didn't apologize or retract his story.

"You're a whore with scars on your back," he said.

And as with the NBA star, this was a story that would plague the rest of our time together. Every time we fought, he brought it up as yet more evidence against me. I was beginning to see that there was nothing I could do to change his mind, so I just tried harder to keep the peace.

Almost every time Russell got mad at me, he claimed that I had been unfaithful. And any time I had a bruise or mark on my body, he claimed I had gotten it from having violent sex with someone else. This was puzzling to me. Not only was I obviously devoted to Russell, but also there was nothing in our sex life that might have made him think I was into anything like he accused. We never had rough sex. In fact, Russell and I were very traditional in the bedroom. And when things were good between us, our bedroom was a place of intimacy and safety. I think Russell saw those times with me as a way to apologize because he couldn't otherwise find the words.

It got to the point where Russell's rage was so extreme that I began to feel sorry for him. It made me sad that he couldn't see the truth of how much I loved him. And he couldn't seem to control himself, even when he ended up bringing massive trouble down on himself. The fact that I felt sympathetic toward him made me determined to do better.

If I just keep loving him and prove to him that I'm not sleeping with anyone else, and that I'm not ever going to sleep with anyone else, then I can make it right. I can be the first person who loves him unconditionally and doesn't abandon him. And then he'll get better.

I knew that I had a lot to make up for; not only had Russell had an incredibly painful childhood, but also he often told me that he felt like he'd been taken advantage of by the two women who were the mothers of his sons. He was married to his first wife for only eight months. The second woman he had dated for a year, and she had then sued him for $5 million in a palimony lawsuit.

Russell often told me that he thought both of his exes were crazy and recounted dramatic stories to prove his point. He told me that his first wife had been arrested for a DUI while speeding with their son in the car. He said they had fought constantly, with her throwing dishes, and once even cutting the curtains in half while consumed by rage. Russell also told me that she had once tried to knock off his glasses during an argument. When he held out his hand to stop her, her face ran into his palm, and she turned the incident into a domestic violence charge against him. Russell said that his former fiancée had stolen his financial documents and hid them in the wall in their guesthouse. Although these stories were far-fetched—and I eventually came to realize that Russell would embellish or make up stories to make him seem more sympathetic in my eyes—I believed all of them, as I did nearly everything that Russell told me. I wanted to believe him, which made it easier.

Within the first month or two of my relationship with Russell, I ran into his former fiancée, who was the mother of his second son. I was going into a bagel store in Brentwood Village as she and her mother were coming out. When I saw her, I felt nervous, because I knew that she and Russell were constantly fighting with each other, and he had often told me all about what a terrible, manipulative person she was. I thought she might say something rude to me or make a scene. But when she saw me, she smiled in a not unfriendly way.

"You seem like a nice girl," she said. "You should run for the hills."

I kept a smile on my own face, unsure how to respond.

"Also, you can rest assured that if you're driving, especially if you're driving his car, he's recording you."

And then she was gone.

In my naïveté, I dismissed her warning as more evidence that she was just a scorned ex who was crafty and conniving and willing to say anything to get me upset. I never mentioned the incident to Russell.

It was true that Russell was very jealous and it led him to want to know everything about me. When we were first getting to know each other, he used to ask me endless questions. And he would press for greater and greater detail, almost in an investigative sort of way, as if he were trying to dig up dirt on me or catch me not telling him the truth about something. Sometimes when we were out to dinner, he would question me about a very specific detail from my past.

"So how long did you live in Sunrise Harbor?" he asked.

"About a year," I said, while trying to remember if I had ever told him the name of the building in which I had lived in Fort Lauderdale. Since it was just another South Florida highrise that most people outside of the city had never heard of, I was a little puzzled by this detailed question.

I soon found out the source of all the specifics Russell so often quizzed me about. He showed me that he had done a background check on me and printed out pages upon pages of information about me, including former addresses where I had lived, and the names of my neighbors during those times. The only thing missing was my blood type. And then, while looking for a file in our home office one day, I came across an open screen on his computer, which revealed that he had used a service called US Search to look up my license plate number. Maybe he thought my car was cheating on him, too.

Russell told me that he had access to this search service, which allowed him to find out anything about anyone, because he worked with a client who was in the CIA. It had never crossed my mind to do a background check on anyone. I didn't have the desire to have such detailed information on anyone in my personal life, and frankly, I found it a little bit creepy. But at that point I was up for anything that Russell needed to do to feel secure being with me. Again, instead of seeing a red flag, I let Russell explain all of this away.

"I'm just trying to get to know you because I've been burned," he said. "I just want to make sure that I know everything about you so I don't get myself in another situation with a gold digger."

This seemed a little paranoid to me, but it did make sense, after the palimony lawsuit he had been through, and especially in a town such as Beverly Hills, where there were plenty of gold diggers. And most of his questions seemed harmless enough. I knew that I had lived a pretty boring life until then, and if he wanted to talk about every address and every neighbor, that was fine with me. It did make me a little uneasy, though, because it seemed like he was looking for any reason not to trust me and to justify ending our relationship, which, of course, was my biggest fear. And so I kept hoping that once he got to know me, he would finally start to trust me and realize I would never do anything to hurt him. And excluding a lie detector test and a blood sample, there was nothing he didn't research about me. He had even gone so far as to pose as a potential employer, and had called the college I had attended to get information about me. I knew this was odd behavior by any stretch of the imagination. But because I was doing everything possible to maintain my belief that Russell was as perfect as I had thought when I first fell for him, I let it go.

I was thrilled when, after a month or two, Russell made it clear that he wanted to take our relationship to the next level. I was at his house one day, and he was talking to me while I took a bath.

"I want to take care of you," he said. "I don't want you to have to worry about anything."

Here was the knight in shining armor he often was to me. And when we decided that I should move into his house, I was overjoyed.

About a week after we moved in together, I was at the house, trying to get into my routine of doing work from home while Russell was at his office in the Century City neighborhood of Los Angeles. I was talking on the phone with Dwight while trying to print something out from the computer Russell and I shared. The printer wasn't communicating with the computer, so I crawled under the desk to disconnect and reconnect the printer, in hopes that I could make it work. When I was down on the floor, I looked up and saw that two hooks had been nailed into the underside of the desk and that they held a recording device, which was turned on and taping.

I froze. What I was seeing didn't make any sense. I told Dwight that I would have to call him back and hung up.

When I looked closer, I saw that the current file was the fifth of five files. I couldn't make any sense of what I was seeing, and I took the recording device down without really thinking about what I was doing. At first I actually thought that maybe Russell didn't know it was there. And then, when that didn't seem possible, I figured that it couldn't have anything to do with me. Maybe it was something Russell used for work. But when I stopped the recorder and played the files, they were all audio recordings of me.

I started to shake. And cry.

I stood up with the recorder in my hand and walked from the office into the bathroom, where I started to pace. I looked up and caught sight of my reflection and the distraught expression on my face. I almost didn't recognize myself. The whole situation was so surreal. This couldn't be my life.

Oh, my God, I live with this man, and he's recording me. What have I gotten myself into?

I was scared, and I needed an answer from the man I loved.

When Russell answered my call, he could tell I was crying.

"What's wrong?" he asked.

"I found this recording device under the desk," I said. "Did you put it there?"

"Calm down," he said.

"Tell me the truth," I pleaded.

"It's not that big of a deal," he responded.

Finally the truth came out.

"Yes, I just don't know you that well," he said. "I really want to get to know you. I've been burned in the past, and I just felt like this would be an easier way for me to get to know everything about you more quickly."

Hearing all of this made me cry harder.

"I don't understand why you don't trust me," I said. "I know that you've been through a lot with other people, but this really hurts my feelings."

"Well, it won't ever happen again," he said. "But if you're not doing anything wrong, I don't know why you care. You can record me all you want, because I'm not doing anything wrong."

As usual, he knew just what to say to convince me. His logic did make sense to me, and I knew that I had nothing to hide. The problem, of course, was that Russell could always make something out of nothing.

"You said to Dwight earlier in the week that his contractor on his condo was cute," Russell continued.

I couldn't believe that he'd found a way to come home and retrieve and listen to the recordings at night without me realizing it.

"He's *gay*," I said. "The contractor's gay, and I was saying it for Dwight because Dwight's gay."

"You said he was cute."

"He's gay."

Russell didn't care that he had heard only one side of what was a totally innocent conversation. He had found the perfect way to flip the blame from him for recording me, to me, for being recorded.

"You're obviously into this contractor," he said.

"What are you talking about? I said. "Dwight brought up the contractor, and as he was telling me about him, I said he was cute—not for me—for Dwight. You have the wrong idea. If you could have heard both sides of the conversation, you would understand. But since there was only a recorder on one end, you're confused. Please don't be mad. This is silly."

"This isn't going to work," he said. "You should just move out."

Now he had my attention.

And so, once again, I went along with whatever he said, to keep us together. It wasn't until after I hung up that I thought about his ex-fiancée's warning, and I realized that what she had said was true. This meant that Russell was probably recording me in my car, too. For the next nearly six years, I always assumed I was being recorded in the car and at home. In fact, one of our housekeepers later told me that she had seen a small tape recorder under a side table in our bedroom. Of course, I was always careful to make sure the content of my conversations was very clear. And more often than not, there was nothing much for Russell to hear anyhow. I can't even imagine how many hours he must have spent over the years listening to me singing in the car, as well as the audio from Kennedy's Disney DVDs. Soon enough, being listened to by Russell became the norm. And today I sometimes forget that there is no one listening anymore.

Years after I found the first recorder, I was getting dressed one day when I glanced over at the computer screen. I could see that a web browser was open to my e-mail account. Even though I was across the room, the cursor was moving over the screen. I had no idea how that was possible, and it completely freaked me out. This was a new computer, and we had just taken it to our computer guy so he could load on all of the software. My first thought was that our tech guy had installed something to let him hack into our files.

Then I looked more closely. All of the e-mails were mine, but the account wasn't in my name; it was "admenservices." Although I was puzzled, I was also a bit amused. Russell was a terrible speller, and I immediately knew that he was the culprit because he had so clearly misspelled the abbreviation for the word "administrator." I remembered that Russell used a program that allowed him to log into our home computer remotely from his office to retrieve files he had worked on at home. Of course: he was reading my e-mail. Even once I understood what was happening, it was unsettling to watch the cursor go through my e-mails and know that Russell was reading my e-mails while sitting at his computer in his office. I decided to call him and see what he would say.

"We need to get the computer guy over here right now," I said. "Or we need to call the police on the computer guy because he's clearly hacked into my e-mail."

"Oh, you're crazy," Russell said. "It's nothing."

"No, we need to have the computer guy arrested," I said, hoping that if I pushed Russell, he would admit that it had been him all along.

"Well, I don't know," Russell said. "We'll talk about it later."

Russell kept making light of my fears, and nothing ever came of the situation, but I think he knew I was on to him because it was so uncharacteristic of me to say that we should have someone arrested. Normally I was so meek and mild. Not that my bluffing caused Russell to change his behavior at all. I later went into my e-mail settings and found that he had set it up so that all of my e-mails were forwarded to him the moment I received them. I didn't change the setting or confront him. I knew he was going to do what he wanted to do no matter how I reacted. In addition, a part of me had come to believe him that if I didn't have anything to hide, it didn't make a difference if he violated my privacy.

At about the same time when I moved in with Russell, he began taking steps to distance me from any control or knowledge of our finances, under the guise of taking care of me. Because of Russell's story about how his ex had stolen his financial documents, it made some sense to me that Russell was paranoid about his money.

I was willing to go along with anything Russell wanted to make the relationship work and to avoid setting him off. And I just kept telling myself that once he got to know me, all of the suspicion and rage would go away. He'd realize I was a nice girl who loved him and we'd be happy.

My friends and family weren't so convinced. Not long after Russell and I moved in together, I got a phone call from my mother. She told me that Dwight had called her and expressed concerns about my safety. He had not only been on the phone with me the night that I chased Russell down to Manhattan Beach after Russell left me at the Four Seasons, but Dwight had also heard the stories about Russell accusing me of sleeping with the NBA player, having delusions about the scars on my back in Miami, and recording my conversations. Each time I had confessed what was happening, Dwight had told me to leave Russell. And each time I had made excuses for Russell's behavior.

My mother is the sweetest person in the world, so I knew she must be really concerned to get involved like this.

"Dwight says that the person you're with isn't being good to you," my mother said.

Instead of being relieved that they cared enough to get involved, I felt betrayed and went into my default mode of protecting Russell.

"It's fine," I said. "You're overreacting."

The more she pushed, the more defensive I became.

"He's really worried about you," my mom said.

"I don't appreciate you guys meddling in my relationship," I said.

I was in too deep already to get out, even when the people who loved me most tried to offer me a life raft. And soon Russell drew me in even deeper. In the months before I started dating him, it had become increasingly clear that I was going to need to move my textile business to China if I wanted it to remain financially viable. No one was really manufacturing in the United States anymore because the margins were so poor. This was a big step that would have required me to take out a business loan for the substantial outlay of money necessary to get the new venture up and running. Because Russell was a successful venture capitalist, he seemed like the perfect person to advise me. After looking through my books, he said he felt like it wouldn't be a good use of the $500,000 or so it would take to make the switch, and that we could better invest that money in another venture. Even with my business based in China, it would never be that profitable because the profit margins on textiles are not very high. So he suggested that I shut down my business, and I agreed.

And then, after we had been dating for about three months and living together for maybe one, Russell started talking to me about having a baby. I had always been neutral on the subject of kids. I felt like I would be happy if it happened for me, but it wasn't one of my goals in life. I knew I could have an enjoyable, fulfilled life without children. I had quickly come to love Russell's boys, and I felt like a family during the time we spent together, but I hadn't really thought about having a baby of our own. As usual, Russell had strong feelings on the matter and soon set out to make me see things his way.

"You just have to become a mother," he said. "You're just so loving and caring. It would be a shame for you to go through life without being able to give your love to a child."

I was flattered by his words, but I still wasn't so sure. I didn't feel like I had the skill set to be a mother. I was keenly aware that I hadn't been raised in very good surroundings. I didn't have siblings, and I'd never babysat, so I'd never even changed a diaper. Plus, I had always been focused on being able to support myself and make sure I never became a single mother who had to struggle like my mother had.

When I didn't agree right away, Russell kept bringing it up. "With all you've been through with your own family, it would just be a shame for you not to have a family of your own," he said.

Wow, maybe I could be a mother, I thought.

But I still wasn't completely convinced.

"It would be a disservice to children everywhere for you not to be a mother to one of them, and to love them the way that you love me," he said.

It felt so good to finally hear him acknowledge the love I was so aware of doing everything in my power to give to him. He had me.

We got pregnant right away, and by this point I really wanted the baby and was overjoyed at the news. Russell was never someone to get overly emotional about anything, but he seemed happy in his own way.

He took a picture of the pregnancy test stick with its positive result. We had a business dinner that night, and he brought the camera with him and showed it to everyone.

There was just one catch.

Russell only wanted to keep the baby if it was a girl, because he already had two boys. Russell had me so completely in his control by then that I never would have jeopardized our relationship, even for something I had now come to want so badly for myself. At five weeks I took a blood test and mailed in the sample to learn the gender, and fate, of our baby. I was a nervous wreck for the next week or two as I waited for the results. Finally I received an e-mail: there was 99.8 percent chance that the baby was a girl. When I read this, I started to cry.

I called Russell at the office, still crying, to tell him the news.

"That's great," he said.

Although the baby had been Russell's idea, and he was very supportive when it came to the idea of having a daughter, that's where his involvement and interest in the pregnancy stopped.

I called him, crying, from my car during a particularly rough day in the middle of my pregnancy.

"I'm just emotional today," I said. "I just feel all of these hormones, and I feel so alone."

"You are alone," he said. "You're the only one that's pregnant. I've got to go."

When he hung up on me, just like that, I felt more isolated than ever. But as Russell had trained me to do, I told myself that I was overreacting, and buried my feelings even deeper, so that my pregnancy wouldn't affect him. But at what should have been the happiest moment in our relationship, his rage began to intensify, and I soon had even more severe feelings of loneliness and sadness to bury.

chapter five

Pizza without a Vegetable

We did have some moments of closeness during my pregnancy. When Russell came home from work, he would ask me about my day.

"What did you do all day?" he would say.

"I created a human life," I'd reply. "What did you do today?"

He would always smile when he heard me say that.

"Well, I did a couple of deals, but I guess you've got me there."

In addition to being pregnant, I actually had plenty to keep me busy. During our first summer together, it had become clear that the commute between our home in Manhattan Beach and Russell's business meetings, and my doctor's appointments in Los Angeles wasn't working out anymore. We found a modern three-story house in Laurel Canyon that had a small room off the master bedroom that we could use as a nursery when the baby was born. I threw myself into the move and getting our new home ready for the baby. At the same time, I was still accompanying Russell when he went out in the city or traveled for business dinners and meetings, and his calendar had not quieted at all.

Even though Russell was never emotional or demonstrative, I felt closer to him than ever. We had moved into a new house together where we were starting our new family, we had talked about getting married, and things seemed to be moving along in our relationship. But as I soon learned, Russell almost seemed to grow uncomfortable when we became too intimate, and many of our best moments together were followed by our worst.

We had fallen into a pattern where Russell lashed out at me about every six weeks. Usually, as I could feel us getting closer, conflict would arise. I don't think he was conscious of the pattern, and I certainly wasn't at the time, but it was almost as if he could feel himself letting his guard down, so he would create some scenario whereby he could push me away and create emotional distance between us to protect himself from feeling too much. In the late summer or early fall of 2005, when I was about three or four months pregnant, Russell first showed me what he was really capable of doing to me.

One evening I was in our Laurel Canyon home's master bedroom, which was on the bottom floor. His mother and sons were upstairs in the kitchen and main area, above which were the boys' bedrooms and a guest room. Russell and I were attending a charity event that night, so I had cooked a pizza for his boys for dinner and then gone downstairs to prepare myself for the evening out. I had already dressed in a short brown maternity dress with an empire waist, and I was going back and forth between the bathroom and my closet, getting myself ready.

Russell arrived home from work and came downstairs. Before I knew what was happening, he grabbed me by my throat and shoved me against the wall right next to the bathroom door. I was instantly shaking, and panting, and trying to figure out what had set him off because he was so angry—as mad as I'd ever seen him—and I had no idea why. I knew he hadn't been drinking, since he'd just returned from the office. He held me up against the wall by my neck with his right hand and brought his face very close to mine.

"If you ever again serve my kids a pizza without a vegetable, I'll kill you," he said. "You have just humiliated me in front of my mother."

I was so scared and upset that I started to cry a little.

"I'm so sorry," I said. "I'm sorry."

He made a sound of disgust as he let go of me and moved away.

"You're such a wounded lamb," he said. "You just crumble at every little thing."

I didn't dare to apologize again but I couldn't stop crying. That just made him angrier.

"You're such a baby," he said. "Go cry in the corner."

He moved over to his closet to change into a fresh suit.

"You know what? I'm just going to go to this event by myself. I'm not even going to take you," he said.

Being left behind was even worse than getting yelled at or choked. Even though he had just been physically violent with me for the first time in our relationship, I wanted nothing more than to be close to him. Pregnancy could feel isolating enough without being left at home by an angry partner.

"Please, I want to go," I begged. "Please don't go without me."

He didn't ever say that he would take me, but I finished getting ready, and he let me go with him to the charity event after all. Not that he talked to me all night; he was clearly still very angry, and he ignored me throughout the event. And for no good reason, either—when I first met Russell, he was feeding his boys microwaved fish sticks for dinner, so it's not like they were used to eating gourmet meals.

I thought back to the incident with the scars in Miami, and again I wondered if Russell had some sort of a mental imbalance because he would get so incredibly angry about the most insignificant—or even invented—things. I used to say that it was as if his thermostat were off, because in situations where a normal, rational person would not have been upset at all, he became irrationally, uncontrollably angry. But then I would think back to Russell's childhood and all he had been through. It seemed to me that he was right to be so defensive; that he had programmed himself to respond like he did as a protective mechanism from when he was little. I knew the good side— the side that loved me—and felt for him that he had been given so many reasons to distrust others.

All he needs is unconditional love, and eventually he will soften. Eventually he will change.

I was already afraid of Russell by that point because the verbal abuse had gotten so bad after we moved in together. But after he choked me, instead of thinking about getting away, I became even more determined to stay on top of everything—from always serving the kids a vegetable with dinner, to how I behaved when we were out—to try to make sure he never had a reason to hurt me again. Russell would become furious if he was looking for a particular shirt to wear to the office and it was at the dry cleaner's. If it had been cleaned, but I had neglected to pick it up, that could set him off for the day. I set out to make sure this never happened again. I was living under the myth that if I controlled Russell's surroundings, I could keep him under control.

But when Russell was happy, those were among the happiest times of our life together—and of my life in general. Together we prepared for little Kennedy to join our family. I prepared to be a mother by decorating the nursery in cream and yellow and picking out the tiniest clothes imaginable. We celebrated the holidays together for the first time, starting traditions such as shopping for our Christmas tree at Mr. Green Trees and decorating it with the boys. Wherever we went, we took pictures. Russell was the only guy I've ever met who always had a camera ready to capture special moments and loved having photos of our precious memories. For one of our later Christmases together, he gave me several leather photo albums filled with memories of our life together from the time we started dating. Although he laughed as he confessed to having his assistant arrange the albums, the idea had been his, and it had been something special that he had wanted me to have forever. In those moments I knew how much he loved me, while recognizing that it wasn't easy for him to show it. I was able to forgive and forget and hope our happiness lasted a lifetime. But unfortunately, every six weeks our happiness faded as Russell lashed out at me once again.

I did, thankfully, find a source of outside support while I was pregnant, and right around the time when Russell's abuse escalated from verbal to physical. And it gave me the perspective to know that it was typical for abuse to intensify like that, once the abuser wasn't getting the same level of reaction from the verbal attacks anymore. The previous year, I had met Carol Adelkoff, the CEO of the 1736 Family Crisis Center, at a charity event. She and I instantly hit it off, and I was incredibly moved by the passion she dedicated at the center's five shelters to helping families who had faced domestic violence. Obviously, because of my family history, I was well aware of the importance of such work and decided to get involved. By the time I did my first shelter visit, when I was pregnant with my daughter, I clearly had even more reason to be drawn to the center's mission. I wasn't conscious of any motivation at the time, beyond wanting to give back to these women and their children, but I think it was comforting for me to be there with them and that I benefited from hearing their stories and the messages they were given by the marriage and family therapists who were there to help them. I always felt incredibly connected to the women I met there, and I'm sure a good deal of that came from my experience with Russell. I think it was reassuring for me to hear that these women, too, suffered from low self-esteem and an inability to believe they deserved better, which led them not only to be unable to leave for so long, but also to believe that they had actually caused the abuse.

And I think it was particularly heartening to me that eventually they had all gotten out.

Although it had been Russell's idea to have a baby, I had mixed feelings about what kind of father he would be. I knew that he adored his boys. He loved spending time with them, and taking them to do fun things such as going to batting cages or the go-kart track. I never saw an instance where he was verbally or physically abusive to either of them, and he even seemed to take precautions not to yell in front of them. I took this to mean that his anger would continue to be directed only at me, and that our baby would be safe from any harm.

At the same time, Russell loved his work. He was a complete workaholic, which left very little time for anyone in his life, including me. He worked long hours, and even when he got home late, he often went right into his home office and logged on to his computer. I could tell that the boys didn't always get as much attention from him as they would have liked when they were at our house. But Russell had big dreams for our family's future, and he was going to work as hard as he could to make them happen.

But Russell did have experience being a dad, and I figured that would be helpful, since I'd spent so little time with babies. Of course, Russell had told me right up front that he did not plan to be a hands-on dad and he did not change diapers.

Russell's attendance at my Lamaze classes became such a joke that Russell and I actually turned it into a funny bit that we shared with friends. He showed up an hour and a half late to the first class and didn't come to the second class at all.

When he sneaked into the third class late and sat down next to me, I thought I was going to be sick. He reeked of whiskey, and I was very sensitive to the smell of alcohol throughout my pregnancy. It was embarrassing at the time, especially because I was sure that the other attendees could tell something was up with my marriage. But I could laugh about it later when I realized how little I remembered about Lamaze once I was in labor. And Russell and I joked that while all of the other husbands were sitting beside their wives and rubbing their shoulders during class, I had a name tag sitting beside me each week.

When it came time for the last class and its hospital tour, during which we would learn where Russell would bring me when I went into labor, he still hadn't arrived. My Lamaze teacher wrote him a note to tell him where we would be and left it on the classroom door.

"He's always late," I said. "It's okay."

"As long as he's nice to you otherwise," she said.

I was embarrassed that she had such a low opinion of our marriage after only four classes. Of course, if she had known how far he was from nice to me, she probably would have felt moved to intervene on my behalf.

Because my mother did know the true nature of my relationship with Russell, I didn't want to tell her that I was having a child with him, and I put it off for as long as possible. Finally, when I was five months along, and showing, I realized it had to be done.

I asked her to meet me for lunch at The Ivy on Robertson,

and I arrived early to get everything ready. I made sure there were extra pillows around the banquette where she would be sitting, in case she passed out. When she arrived, I ordered her a glass of champagne. Now, my mother does not drink, but I knew how hard this was going to be for her, so I was going all out. I handed my mom a wrapped gift. Inside was a Tiffany frame that contained a picture of a sonogram showing my baby sucking her thumb. At first my mom looked confused.

"That's your granddaughter," I said. "I'm pregnant."

My mother started to cry with happiness.

"Well, how long have you been trying?" she asked.

"Two martinis and forty-five minutes," I said.

Of course, my mom was instantly supportive of me and could not have been more thrilled that she was going to be a grandmother. But she and my stepdad remained somewhat distant from Russell, who didn't help matters by rarely making eye contact with them. I think he worried that they knew about his abuse, and he often asked me later in our relationship if they knew what had transpired between us during darker times.

But regardless of how worried my mother might have been about Russell's treatment of me, I wasn't only thinking about myself just then. I had a baby on the way. Since I had shut down my business, I had no means of supporting her or me. And Russell continued to give me reason to hope.

That summer, we took his youngest son, Griffin—who was five at the time—out to dinner one night. We went to Locanda Portofino, a wonderful Italian restaurant tucked away next to a Laundromat and a convenience store in a strip mall in Santa Monica. As we settled into our table and placed our orders, Griffin walked around to where Russell was sitting. They made a quick handoff under the table, and I assumed they were just playing. But then Griffin returned to my side of the table with an engagement ring.

"Will you marry me?" Russell said.

I looked up at Russell, my expression filled with happiness. "Yes, of course," I said. "I love you. I'm so excited."

NOT THAT ALL OF Russell's surprises were such cause for celebration. Right before our wedding, Russell took me out to lunch.

"I have to tell you something," he said, sounding serious.

"What is it?" I asked.

"I filed for bankruptcy," he said.

"What do you mean?" I asked.

"This palimony lawsuit is not going away," he said. "It's a frivolous claim. And I've been advised to file for bankruptcy."

Of course, I later found out that the palimony lawsuit was far from the only source of financial trouble in Russell's life, but at that point I still believed everything he told me. The fact that I never hesitated to marry him, even though he was bankrupt at the time, should have reassured him that I was anything but a gold digger. But of course, nothing could ever seem to put Russell's paranoia to rest.

I don't know if it was Russell's admitted history of bad relationships, or the fact that I'd seen too many cop dramas, but
his obsession with investigating me began to make me suspicious that something more was going on with him than he'd let
on. I was several months pregnant when Russell approached
me with his next detective scheme: he decided that I should go
to downtown Los Angeles and be fingerprinted by a company.
Yes, fingerprinted. Then my fingerprints would be sent to both
the Federal Bureau of Investigation and the Department of
Justice. He also requested copies of my birth certificate, U.S.
passport, driver's license, and driving record for the past ten
years. Now, downtown LA is not the easiest place to navigate,
especially for a tired, pregnant woman whose feet feel as big as
Fred Flintstone's. But to ease Russell's suspicions, downtown I
went, pregnant and puzzled, and got myself fingerprinted. The
company sent the prints directly to the FBI and the Department of Justice. Meanwhile, I asked for my driving records
from the DMV and made photocopies of the documents Russell had requested. Then we waited.

Within a few weeks, Russell had everything on me that
he felt he needed. No criminal records had been found for
anyone with my fingerprints—shocking! I don't know if he
thought I was on the lam from Rikers Island, or what. I sup-
pose the investigation gave Russell the peace of mind about
me that he had lacked. All I got was the paperwork, which I've
kept in a neat little spiral binder; black fingertips; and a very
uneasy feeling. I continued to make excuses for Russell at the
time, but looking back, I can see that I should have known that

such a deep paranoia must have come from something much darker than a few past relationships gone awry.

IN OCTOBER 2005, RUSSELL and I got married at the One&Only Palmilla in Los Cabos, Mexico, which had always been one of our favorite places to vacation together. On a previous trip, we had walked up to the property's old Spanish chapel, and Russell said that if we ever got married we should have the ceremony there. When we traveled back to the resort for our wedding when I was five months pregnant, I thought about how much hope I had felt during that earlier visit. The day of the ceremony, as we lounged by the pool, I felt far from hopeful. In fact, I had a sense of foreboding. I knew in my heart that this marriage wasn't a good idea and that the wedding probably shouldn't be happening. But I already loved Russell so deeply that it was impossible for me to walk away, and I didn't know how I would ever be able to make it without him. It may have been an unhealthy, codependent love, but I didn't know how to have any other kind.

But then Russell surprised me as he sometimes did, and made me think that maybe everything *would* turn out happily ever after.

The ceremony was beautiful and intimate—just the two of us—and held at dusk. I rode in a horse-drawn carriage to the chapel, which was perched on a hill atop a dramatic stone staircase and surrounded by palm trees. I had sent David Yurman cuff links and studs to Russell's room, and he wore them with a black tux.

After we exchanged our rings, while we still stood at the altar, Russell pulled out a necklace. I was expecting the kind of standard gift a husband might normally give his new wife— diamond earrings or a bracelet—but instead he held a white gold cross on a chain. At the top, he had engraved his initial; on one side was his son Aiden's initial, and on the other, his son Griffin's initial. In the center was mine. As Russell put the necklace around my neck, he uttered the most romantic words he ever said to me throughout the course of our relationship.

"I need you to be the glue that holds our family together," he said.

Then he told me that he had even tried to do the engraving himself. This gesture was so out of character for him, as was the deep sentiment, and I felt incredibly moved. No matter how dark things got, I have always believed that this moment said a great deal about all that Russell wanted our marriage to be. It really felt like a new start for me—and us—and I think he felt the same way. Out of everything he ever did for me, this gift always meant the most to me, because it showed me how much he did love me and because it revealed his sensitive side.

When our daughter, Kennedy Armstrong, was born on February 25, 2006—just one year and eleven days after our first date—we put her initials at the bottom of the cross, and our family was complete.

While Russell was not a hands-on dad, he still expected to control many of the decisions we made about raising our daughter. During all of the reading and preparation I did before giving birth, I kept hearing that it was healthier for babies to breast-feed. I assumed that's what we would do. Russell had a different idea. He thought breast-feeding was gross.

"A woman's breasts are made for a bikini," he said with a hint of sarcasm, trying to gauge my reaction. He occasionally said things—especially sexist comments—to see if he could get me riled up in a playful way. But I knew he was serious about this.

"Really?" I said, unable to believe what I was hearing but not wanting to confront him directly.

Russell went on to explain that if he saw me breast-feeding our daughter, he thought it would be hard for him to think of my breasts in a sexual way after that. Overall, he was firmly opposed to the idea. I just listened, speechless.

By the time Kennedy was born, my breasts looked nothing like the ones I had once put in my bikini, and frankly, I didn't feel like I would ever want to have sex again; so bring on the breast-feeding. I wanted to do what was best for our baby. And so for the first few days after Kennedy was born, I tried to breast-feed, no matter how adamant Russell was about his opinion. He was at the office for all but her nighttime feedings, which I did in her nursery and out of view of Mr. Bikini Contest. But as any new mom knows, breast-feeding is not always the easiest thing to master, and I was on the verge of giving up when Australia came to my rescue.

Two or three days after Kennedy was born, Russell went on a trip to Australia. I had a live-in baby nurse at the house with me, and during the time he was away, I was able to finally get the hang of it. By the time Russell was scheduled to return, I was doing really well with the breast-feeding, and Kennedy seemed healthy and happy. I thought I might try to convince Russell of the benefits breast-feeding would have for our daughter.

But I never had the chance. The minute—literally—that his plane landed in Los Angeles, I stopped producing milk. Even when I tried to pump, and stayed on the machine forever, I would end up with the tiniest amount of milk that wasn't even enough to supplement with formula. So I had to stop breast-feeding, and Kennedy went on formula.

My baby nurse had been trained by the woman who wrote *The Baby Whisperer* and had worked with new moms for thirty years, and she said she had never before seen that kind of psychological reaction to another human being. Of course, I wasn't surprised that Russell maintained such complete control over me, and my body, even when he wasn't in the room.

Once Kennedy was born, I became even more devoted to my marriage. At that point I almost felt like I couldn't live without Russell. I remembered how tough it was being raised without a father, and I was determined to avoid re-creating that childhood for Kennedy. As far as I was concerned, it was better for Kennedy to have a dad, so she wouldn't share my abandonment issues and low self-esteem, no matter the personal cost my marriage might exact on me.

Of course, looking back, I realize that it was worse for Kennedy to be raised around abuse than divorce, or anything else. But at the time I really believed that I would be able to shield her from the worst of Russell's outbursts, and I was mostly successful. I also think that it was difficult for me because I didn't want to be a struggling single mom, so I was just glad to have a man in my life, no matter what. Russell did his part to grow my fears of what life would be like without him.

"If you leave, you'll be out on the street," he said. "I won't take care of you. You and Kennedy will be living in a cardboard box."

For a few months immediately after Kennedy was born, our life together was relatively calm, without any dramatic outbursts. I was learning to be a mommy—little sleep and lots of joy—and enjoying getting to know my beautiful little girl. I will always cherish the special moments that the three of us shared during that time, especially seeing Kennedy asleep on Russell's chest. She looked so small, and he looked so strong and protective of her. As a baby, Kennedy slept with her arms above her head, just like her daddy. And still, to this day she snores, just like him. Russell and I often joked that she would live with us forever, since her snoring would run off any potential suitors.

Of course, Russell still kept a tight control over all aspects of my life. At first he had established a rule that if I spent $500 or less, I didn't have to clear it with him, as long as I didn't buy several $500 items on the same day. But then he began scrutinizing my credit card bill every month. It reached the point where, anytime I entered his office and saw my American Express statement on the computer screen, I would become incredibly nervous. Sometimes I felt like it wasn't the money I had spent that Russell was concerned about, so much as how his insanely jealous personality led him to want a detailed accounting of each and every moment of my life.

"Who were you with at Il Pastaio?" he would ask.

"What?" I would reply.

"You had lunch there on March twentieth," he would say. "Who were you with?"

I would search my memory for the lunch in question, knowing that if I couldn't provide him with an accurate and detailed description he would most likely fly into a rage and accuse me of cheating.

I think it was important to Russell that I looked good, but he wasn't concerned about me wearing certain designers as a sign of status or anything like that. What was more likely to set him off was if he thought a dress made me look too thin, or was going to get too much attention when we went out. And then, as with every other time he was unhappy with me, Russell could be terribly blunt and cruel.

A few months after Kennedy was born, we traveled back to Mexico as a family, this time to Las Ventanas. I was so happy to be on vacation, and back in the country where we had gotten married. And it felt amazing not to be pregnant anymore and to have our beautiful baby girl in our lives. One night, Russell and I had plans to go out to dinner, just the two of us. I dressed carefully in a green halter dress with Spanish embellishments that I had bought for the trip. I felt good in it, especially now that I was no longer pregnant. When Russell and I got into the car to go to the restaurant, he looked over at me.

I smiled at him, feeling like we were in a good place.

"You look like a whore," he said.

And just like that, I deflated. With my happiness went the possibility I had felt that we were headed in the right direction and that things were going to change between us. Looking back, I feel like this was another case where Russell found himself growing too close to me and had to push me away with meanness. I've since heard other abused women speak about these cycles of affection and violence, and also how their husbands would brag about them in public, only to tear them down behind closed doors. That was definitely a pattern for Russell and me. Whatever the reason things got like they did, I didn't feel good about it.

Russell continued to stay very busy with his business, and I was completely devoted to being the best mother I could be to our daughter. While I spent my days attending to Kennedy, because I had a live-in nanny I was able to accompany Russell to many dinners and meetings, much as I had always done. When Russell and I were out together, I always policed my behavior carefully to make sure I didn't do anything to offend him.

And, of course, when I was out without Russell, I had to be extremely careful to remain available to him at all times. When Kennedy was about a year old, I went out one night with my friend Linda Thompson, the singer/songwriter who is perhaps best known for having dated Elvis. She invited me out to a charity event for the Chrysalis Foundation at Saks Fifth Avenue. It was a shopping event, and we were having such a nice night, and running into so many interesting people because Linda knows everyone in town.

We next went to the Beverly Wilshire Hotel to have dinner at Cut, which is owned by Linda's friend Wolfgang Puck. He came over and joined us at our table. We then saw another of her friends, Lionel Richie, who also joined us. Soon we had this great table, and we were all having so much fun. By this point in my relationship with Russell, I knew enough to take out my phone and put it on the table in front of me when I was out with friends so I could answer instantly, should Russell text or call me. But on this night, I got caught up in the conversation and the laughter, and when I saw that I had a call coming in from Russell, I didn't realize that he had already called me several times. I immediately went outside and called him back, but my stomach was twisted with anxiety.

"I don't know what the fuck you're doing," he said. "I don't know who you're with."

"I'm with Linda," I said. "We're having dinner at Cut."

"You're lying," he said. "You're obviously with someone you don't want me to know about because you're not answering the phone."

Really, I knew that Russell was just jealous that I was out with Linda because, although he really liked her, she intimidated him because she knew so many people and was so well-liked around town. Of course, Russell should have been happy that, out of all of the women in Beverly Hills, I was friends with Linda, who has a flawless reputation, is far from wild, and rarely drinks. But I think Russell was nervous that I might have the opportunity to meet new people through Linda and that he would then lose some of his control over me.

I tried to enjoy the rest of my evening out, but I was nervous about what would happen when I got home. I felt a sense of growing dread as I walked into the house. Of course, Russell was furious and immediately started screaming at me about what a whore I was and how I couldn't be trusted. And he hadn't calmed down by the next morning.

I was holding Kennedy in the living room of the house in Studio City we had moved to that year, when he stalked over to me and threw his wedding ring at me. It hit me in the face and dropped to the floor. Kennedy's head was right next to mine, and he could have easily hit her. But in moments like that, he had no ability to think logically. He walked out the door and slammed it behind him.

I was shaken by the fact that Russell had lashed out at me in front of Kennedy, even though she was only a year old, and I doubted that she would remember the moment. I wanted to talk to one of my friends, but I didn't feel like there was any place from which I could call them without being recorded. I knew that I certainly couldn't talk in my car. So when I was driving later that day, I pulled over in the Beverly Glen Center and got out of the car to call Linda. As I stood in the parking lot and told her what had happened, I started to cry. Even though I was determined to stay with Russell, he didn't make it easy.

And little did I know that our struggle was about to take an even darker turn.

chapter six

"I'm Afraid I'm Going to Kill You"

After a brief period of calm following Kennedy's birth, Russell's physical violence against me escalated. Our relationship was more cemented now, with a marriage and a child, but I felt more uncertain around him than ever. He began using a new tactic where he would grab my hair when we were leaving a party or dinner and bang my head against the side of the car between the two doors, or against the glass of the passenger side window while he was driving, because it made his point to me but didn't leave a visible mark. At the same time that Russell was becoming increasingly brutal, he also had surprising moments of clarity about his behavior toward me. One night after he had beaten the side of my head on the way home, he seemed to feel bad, which was unusual for him. When we were getting ready for bed, he turned to me with an expression of remorse I hadn't seen before.

"The next time I hit you, you should hit me back," he said.

I stared at him in disbelief, but I could tell that he was serious, so I nodded my head.

About a month later, he was banging my head against the window of the car as he drove us home from a party at which I had angered him. I remembered what he had told me, and so I reached over and half hit, half pushed at his face with the palm of my left hand. He stopped banging my head, but when he turned to look at me, his face was flushed and consumed by an expression of pure, murderous rage like I had never seen before. I instantly knew that hitting him was the last thing I ever should have done, even though he had told me to do so. Russell remained quiet during the rest of the ride home, but that was no solace. I knew he could blow up at any moment, and I was terrified.

The next day, Russell mentioned what had happened the night before.

"You know when I told you to hit me back?" he said.

I nodded my head nervously.

"Don't ever do that again because I almost killed you last night," he said. "One of these days, I'm afraid I'm going to kill you."

Russell expressed this fear to me on more than one occasion. It was almost as if he were saying that he was as scared of himself as I was, and that, like me, he feared that the violent urges that surged inside him were beyond his control. As strong as he was, and as much as he did lose himself when swallowed up by his rage, I knew that a good blow to the temple could have been enough to do me in.

One of our worst fights happened after another occasion

when I had been out with Linda Thompson, and she introduced me to one of the founders of MySpace, Chris. A few weeks later, Russell and I attended a holiday party at my friend's house in Bel Air.

Chris saw me and we said hello.

"Oh, hi, Taylor, good to see you again," he said.

"Hi," I said. "This is my husband, Russell."

We made small talk for a moment, and then we parted ways with Chris and went on with our evening. I could tell that Russell was mad, but I couldn't think of what I had possibly done to set him off. By the time we left the party, Russell was fuming. He started in on me as soon as we got outside and away from the other guests. The angry words and the ugly names he chose to call me were the same as always, but by this time, they were having less effect than they had before.

"When you introduced me to that guy, he acted like he didn't even know you were married," he said.

How does a person act when he doesn't know somebody's married? I wondered. *And what should I have done to let him know I was married—other than wearing my wedding ring—given how briefly I'd met him the first time?*

"You didn't tell him that you were married," he raged. "You were obviously with him."

"No, no, I'm sorry," I said. "I don't know if I told him I was married, or not. I didn't even meet him for long enough. But you're right, I should have told him that I'm married. And, I mean, I'll make sure in the future to tell people that I'm married right away."

I was trying to reason with him as he stormed out to our

car, but he was in one of his blind rages. When we got to the car, he grabbed my head and started banging it against the side of the vehicle, as he had done before.

While Russell was driving us home, he reached over with his right hand and kept bashing the side of my head against the car window. Even though we had moved to our house in Bel Air by that point, and it was a short drive home, it felt like it took forever. I have a high tolerance for pain, but Russell really hurt me that night, and I was crying hard. By the time we got home, my head was throbbing, and I had a knot on my skull. But Russell wasn't done with me. When we got inside the house and went up to our bedroom, he kept screaming at me.

Now *I* was to blame for the beating.

"You just make me so angry I can't control myself," he said.

"I'm sorry, Russell," I said, crying hysterically.

"The things you do make me crazy," he said in disgust.

In that moment I completely believed that he was right and that everything he had done to me that night was *my* fault. I had to figure out how to be the person he needed me to be, and not to bring out his anger, so that I didn't have to lose him; that was still my biggest fear.

Eventually I stopped trying to defend myself and silently began getting ready for bed in hopes that we could go to sleep before things escalated any further. But I was having trouble calming down. I could feel that Russell had really injured me, and so when he went into the bathroom, I sneaked into Kennedy's room, where she was asleep with her nanny, Gloria. By this time Gloria had lived with us for three years. She was incredibly devoted to Kennedy and had become like a family member to us. She was older than I—in her fifties—and such a sweet woman.

Gloria knew about Russell's abuse because I often went into Kennedy's room and got into bed with Kennedy after Russell and I fought. Sleeping with my daughter gave me a feeling of security that I never felt sleeping with Russell. On a few occasions, Russell followed me into Kennedy's room and brought me back to our bedroom because he wasn't done yelling at me, but he never did anything to me in front of Kennedy or Gloria.

That night I went over to Gloria's bed and whispered to her so I wouldn't disturb Kennedy. I was fairly choked up because I had been crying quite a bit, but I managed to get her name out.

"Gloria," I said, "Russell's being mean to me again."

I cried softly as I told her the whole story. She predominantly speaks Spanish, and my Spanish is terrible, so she didn't get all the details, but she knew Russell well enough to understand what had happened. She hugged me and started to cry a little bit herself.

Russell had scared me with the violence of his attack, and I had Gloria take pictures of my head, even though it was hard to see the knots on my head through my hair. Finally, totally exhausted, I slid into bed next to my daughter, held her close to me, and fell asleep.

The next day I acted like everything was totally normal in front of Kennedy, even though my head was sore where Russell had banged it, and my eyes were swollen from crying. I felt like I needed to let my friends know what had happened because Russell had really scared me the night before, but I knew I couldn't talk in my car.

While I was driving Kennedy to school, which I did on most days, I called Dwight.

"I need to talk to you," I said. "Are you going to be home later?"

"Yeah. Are you okay?" he said. "What happened?"

"Yeah, I'm fine," I said. "I'm taking Kennedy to school."

Of course, by then he and all of my other friends knew that I couldn't talk in my car. And they could always tell if I was driving when they called me because I'd say the same thing:

"Just give me a minute. Just give me a minute. I'm getting out."

After I dropped Kennedy off, I pulled over at a park near my daughter's school, got out of the car, and called Dwight.

"You need to leave," he said. "He's an asshole. He's crazy. And he's never going to change."

"I know," I said. "But I love him."

We had been having this conversation for years. Dwight always told me to leave, and I always made excuses for why I needed to stay.

"You deserve better than this," Dwight said.

Of course, I didn't believe him about that. But in my head, I would agree that I needed to leave Russell and think that maybe I would really do it this time. But in a day or two I would be right back to feeling like I couldn't leave, not only because I didn't know how I'd take care of Kennedy, but also because I loved Russell and truly didn't think I could live without him. Staying meant doing my best, once again, to convince Russell that I really didn't want to be with anyone but him. I still believed that if I could just make him understand my loyalty and devotion, the abuse would finally stop. During this time I often found myself rubbing my fingers over the cross Russell had given me at our wedding, as if trying to summon the hope and love I had felt in that moment.

Later that day, Gloria came up to me when Kennedy was in her playroom.

"You're so young," she said. "And you have your whole life ahead of you. You need to get out of this relationship. I know because I didn't do those things when I was young, and I gave up my youth. You need to get out now so you can have another life with Kennedy."

I knew she was right, just like Dwight and my other friends were right, but I wasn't ready. I didn't have the strength. I was afraid that I would never meet another man if I left Russell. And to be completely honest, I didn't feel like I deserved to be properly loved and respected. So I just smiled and nodded at Gloria.

"If you ever need me to help you, I will," she said.

"Thank you, Gloria," I said.

Not long after that, Russell started in on me again. This time, I thought I had the perfect ammunition to let him know that he couldn't bully and abuse me anymore.

"Gloria took pictures of my head the other night when you hit it against the car."

Russell reared back and stared at me, trying to see if I was serious.

"Where are they?" he asked.

Of course, I didn't dare have the photos at the house because I was terrified that if Russell found them, he would have become convinced I was plotting against him and have flown into such a catastrophic rage that he would have killed me. Gloria was keeping the photos for me at her house.

"Just don't do it again, or I'll show them to someone," I said.

"Go ahead and tell the police," Russell said defiantly. "If you send me to jail, my business will be ruined. I won't be able to earn a living, and you and Kennedy will end up on the street. I won't give you anything. You'll end up living in a cardboard box. I'll drag you through the courts. I'll bankrupt you. I'll make sure you never see your daughter again."

There was no winning with Russell. And even worse, once Russell knew that Gloria and I had conspired against him, he was careful not to let me be alone with her after a fight. He no longer allowed me the opportunity to confide in Gloria, to make sure I never again had the chance to let her photograph my injuries.

One of the hardest things for me to reconcile myself with by this point in our relationship was the fluctuation in Russell's moods, and the fact that such violent outbursts were often followed by moments when he wanted to be intimate with me. A few days after our last fight, Russell wanted to have sex with me, so he started trying to be gentle. He walked over to where I was standing by the bed and touched me.

"I love you," he said.

It was uncomfortable and confusing for me to allow him to have that kind of closeness when he had just been violent and screamed the nastiest insults at me. But I didn't feel like I had a choice, because I didn't want to make Russell angry all over again, and so I let him have sex with me. I did my best to play into the moment, but it felt scary and unsafe to have this big, strong man who had been so mean hovering above me when I was naked. I knew it could go so badly if he decided to hit me, or bite me—which he had done before when he was mad—instead of kissing me. There were times when I lay there in our bed with tears streaming down my cheeks.

"What are you fucking crying about?" Russell would say. "You're such a baby."

Such insults didn't exactly put me in the mood. As soon as Russell finished, I would roll over and curl up in a ball and go to sleep. I felt absolutely degraded, almost like I was being raped at times. I knew it was an unhealthy dynamic, and I hated that I wasn't able to stand up for myself. Out of everything that happened during my marriage, those moments damaged my self-esteem the most because they made me feel like I didn't value myself at all. And I didn't.

Obviously I was having more subdued sex with Russell than ever by this point, but he remained incredibly paranoid about the possibility that I was having wild escapades with other men. In the winter of 2009, I was getting into the shower one day when Russell noticed a small scab—about the size of a pencil eraser—on my lower back around where the waistline of my jeans would rest. Instantly he began to rage.

"You've got a scab on your back from fucking some guy," he said

"No, it's not," I said. "I swear."

"You're a fucking liar," he said.

The truth was embarrassing, but I would have confessed to anything just then to get him to stop yelling.

"It's from a blemish," I said.

It was true. I had gotten a blemish on my back earlier in the week. It had irritated me because my jeans were rubbing against it while I was driving. So I reached back and started to scratch it, but because I wasn't able to see what I was doing, it started to bleed. Of course, Russell didn't believe me. Who would have made up something like that?! But there was no convincing Russell once he had decided he was right about something I had done. He harassed me about the scab relentlessly after that, and especially when he was mad at me about something else.

Russell's torment had begun to take its toll on me, and I finally admitted that I needed help. I still wanted to believe that my marriage could be saved, but I was beginning to doubt that I could do it on my own. In 2009 I began seeing a therapist. I tried to get Russell to go with me, but he could not be convinced.

"I did therapy," he said. "I did two years of anger management, and it didn't do me any good. This isn't going to help, either."

I knew there was no persuading Russell of something he didn't want to do, so I tried to make the best out of my treatments on my own. But after less than a year my therapist finally gave me her honest opinion of the situation during one of our sessions.

"You can keep coming here, and I can keep taking your

money," she said. "But you need to be in marriage counseling, not individual therapy. All we ever do is talk about your husband, and we're not going to be able to change any of these behaviors without him being on board."

My heart sank. That meant there was nothing she could do for me.

"He won't go," I said. "He's not going to do it."

As I walked out of therapy that day, I was consumed by a feeling of despair. I had wanted to believe that therapy would improve my relationship and how I felt about myself and my life. But it had never seemed like there was enough time in the sessions to discuss all the incidents with Russell during the previous week, let alone delve into the deeper issues underlying his behavior or my decision to stay in the marriage. And now my therapist had essentially told me there was no hope. Not only would Russell never agree to therapy, but I had my doubts about how much therapy could really do for him. He was such a master manipulator that I feared he would twist the truth so successfully that our therapy sessions would end on his terms.

At least something positive and totally unexpected did happen that spring when I got a call from a television producer who was interviewing women for a new *Real Housewives* franchise, to be set in Beverly Hills. Apparently my name had been mentioned a few times to the casting agents who were scouting potential cast members. The producer asked me if I wanted to come in for an interview, and I agreed. I had seen the shows set in several other cities, and it seemed like it could be interesting and fun to be on television. At that point I didn't know if I really wanted the experience. But I believe in taking the opportunities that come our way, and living life in as big a way as possible, so I decided to at least explore the possibility. Of course, I told Russell as soon as I got the call. He didn't seem to think there was any chance that I would get cast, out of all of the women in Los Angeles. He told me to have fun, and that was it.

By the spring of 2009, for more than four years, my friends had been telling me to leave Russell. But I had always managed to justify my decision to stay with him—at least to myself—as long as I was able to control him well enough that no one ever got hurt but me. And then an incident happened on May 22, 2009, that showed me just how foolish I had been to think that I controlled Russell, or his rages, in the slightest.

Russell and I had met up at the W Hotel earlier in the evening to watch a Lakers game on television, and we had been having a great evening. My friend Jennifer had gotten engaged, and she was planning her wedding in Las Vegas for that fall. Her fiancé, Mark, had flown into town that night, and she had invited me over to see him and hear about her latest wedding plans. Jennifer lived one street over from our house in Bel Air, so I decided to visit them on my way home. Russell and I were driving in separate cars, so he stopped over to say hello to Jennifer's fiancé, too.

The four of us sat out on the back patio by Jennifer's pool. She and I talked about her wedding, and she showed me the designs she had picked out, which, of course, Russell couldn't have cared less about. He was a good sport about it for as long as he could be, but he finally decided to go home. And one thing about Russell, as I had learned over the years, was that when he was ready to go, he was ready to go. He would always leave events, parties, and dinners without any explanation or niceties. Since I had my own car, I decided to visit a little longer.

"Okay, I'm going to stay here and hear about the rest of her wedding plans," I said. "I'll meet you at home."

After Russell left, Mark turned to me with a serious expression.

"How are things going?" he asked.

Since Jennifer had been one of my best friends for years, she knew about the abuse, and now Mark did, too.

I tried to smile, but it was hard to deny how bad conditions at my house had become.

"You know, good days and bad days," I said.

I looked at the two of them, sitting there together, looking so happy as they talked about their upcoming wedding. I felt so far away from that feeling of hope and happiness. I stood to go and pulled my keys out of my purse. They walked me toward the gate.

"If anything ever happens to me, just promise me that you guys will take care of Kennedy," I said.

They exchanged a concerned look.

"The fact that you're even worrying about that is a sign that you need to get out of this relationship," Jennifer said.

Mark nodded.

"I'll help you," he said. "If you need it, we'll get you an apartment. We'll do whatever it takes to get you and Kennedy to safety."

"Thanks," I said.

"I mean it," he said. "We're always here for you. If you need an apartment, or whatever you need, we'll help you out."

Just then, we heard a noise over near the gate. There were coyotes in the neighborhood, and Jennifer always worried that they would attack her two pit bulls.

"Oh, my God, Mark, go over there," she said. "It's probably a coyote."

Mark started walking toward the gate. But it wasn't a coyote. All of the sudden, Russell came out of nowhere, talking under his breath.

"You're not going to take my wife away from me," he said. "You're not going to take my wife away from me."

Mark turned back to where we were, but before he could reach us, Russell punched him in the back of the head. Clearly in one of his blind rages, Russell—who was five-nine—grabbed Mark, who was much bigger than Russell—and threw him into the swimming pool. As Mark was trying to climb out of the deep end, Russell bent over the side of the pool, repeatedly punching him. Jennifer and I stood nearby, screaming at Russell to stop.

Russell looked up at me and then he let go of Mark. He jumped up, grabbed me, and threw me into the pool. Then he held my head under the water. Jennifer later told me that she worried, while watching, that Russell had held me under long enough to drown me. Meanwhile, Mark had swum across the pool, and he was emerging from the shallow end. Russell let go of me so he could start fighting with Mark again. Jennifer tried to get between the two men, and Russell threw Jennifer in the swimming pool. And then he threw one of Jennifer's dogs in the pool, too, while the other one barked frantically nearby. Now Jennifer was really screaming because pit bulls can't swim and so her dog had sunk to the bottom of the pool like a brick. While she was rescuing her dog, Russell reached Mark, and once again he punched him—again and again—in the face. Jennifer managed to lift her dog out of the pool and climb out after him, even though her jeans were heavy with water. She ran over, grabbed a fire log, and started swinging at the back of Russell's head to get him to stop. She said that when she looked at Russell, she had never seen anything like it before; there was absolutely no expression on his face—just this vacant, unblinking stare like he was looking right through her—which was exactly what I had seen that night in Miami, and on far too many occasions since then. Jennifer swung the log like a baseball bat and hit Russell in the back of the head.

She's going to kill him, I thought.

But the blows didn't even faze Russell. He kept right on punching Mark. I was trying to pull myself out of the pool, which wasn't easy, because I was wearing a maxi dress and the expanse of fabric was dragging me down. Finally Russell ran through the sliding glass door into the house, and then got in his car and drove away. During the entire fight, Mark hadn't gotten in a single hit. By the time I got out of the pool and reached Jennifer, who was crying as she leaned over Mark, his whole face was completely covered in blood.

We called an ambulance, and while we waited, I couldn't stop crying hysterically and shaking with terror. These people had never seen Russell mad before, but I had, and I knew how out of control he got; I had been certain he was going to kill Mark.

"I'm so sorry," I said again and again.

But in my mind, I was already formulating a plan to protect Russell.

When the police and ambulance arrived, we took Mark to the hospital in nearby Sherman Oaks. Mark's injuries were extensive. I immediately got on my phone and started calling plastic surgeon friends to find someone who could come in that night and sew up his face. Behind me, I could hear Jennifer talking to the police.

"He was trying to drown her," she said, pointing at me. "He was trying to kill her. I'm afraid he's going to kill her."

I wasn't thinking that I had finally been handed my way out from the increasing violence of my marriage. Instead, I was busy trying to determine how I was going to fix this mess to keep my husband out of jail and hold our family together, even though Russell had just tried to drown me and nearly killed my friend's fiancé. Mark's injuries ended up requiring twenty stitches, not to mention the three inches of hair and forehead that Russell had torn off, and five of his front teeth had been knocked out.

When the police questioned me, I tried to give them an account of what had happened without implicating Russell more than I had to.

Oh, my God, he's going to get in big trouble for this one, I thought. *How am I going to get him out of this? What do I need to do to stop this?*

I thought of all of the times Russell had threatened me

with what would happen if he ever ended up in jail, and I was terrified that I wouldn't be able to support Kennedy if he got locked up.

Kennedy was at the house with Gloria, and I felt like I needed to diffuse the situation with Jennifer and Mark, so I ended up staying at Jennifer's house that night. While Jennifer was concerned about my safety, she was furious at Russell, and by extension, at me.

"Now you're letting your problems affect everybody else," she said. "Maybe you're not going to do anything about this, but I'm not going to let somebody treat me like this."

"I'm so sorry," I said.

"Just because this maniac is a part of your life, now he's hurt somebody else," she said.

I knew that she had a point, but I was determined to protect Russell, no matter the cost to me or our friendship.

When I woke up the next morning, before I opened my eyes, I thought, *Please tell me that last night was a nightmare. Please tell me this didn't happen.*

But Jennifer and Mark came into my room almost immediately, and all I had to do was take one look at Mark's face to see just how real—and how bad—the situation was. They were on their way to the cosmetic dentist to talk about repairing his veneers. By this point Mark had recovered from the shock of the night before, and he was furious, too.

Jennifer would barely talk to me. I felt awful. But I didn't have time to wallow in my guilt and fear. I went into crisis management mode. My main concern was still Russell and my family. Our friend Rick had been calling my phone all morning, but I hadn't heard from Russell. After Mark and Jennifer left for the dentist, I finally answered Rick's call. He told me that Russell had gone to his house after the fight.

"Russell told me what happened," he said.

It turned out that Russell had concocted a story about how Mark had started the whole thing. In fact, when he left Jennifer's house that night he had gone straight to the police station to file a complaint against Mark to support his claims, even though he was well aware that the three of us knew exactly what had happened. I think Rick suspected the truth of what had happened that night, but he went along with Russell's story.

"You need to have Russell call me," I said. "I need to help him because he's about to be in big trouble here."

After Rick and I hung up, Russell finally called me.

"You really have done it this time," I said. "I can't cover for you in this situation."

Instead of apologizing or letting on that he was worried about what might happen next, Russell blamed the whole thing on me. According to him, I shouldn't have been talking to my friends about our relationship.

"You're such a crybaby," he said. "That's right, run to all your fucking friends. Go tell everybody how abusive I am and try to get everybody to hate me."

"Russell, you'd better listen to me," I said.

"Fuck you," he said.

"Mark's furious, and he's filed a police report, and they're going to put you in jail," I said.

"Get the fuck out of my life," he said. "If you want to go

get an apartment, and you want Mark to help you, just get the fuck away from me."

"I don't want you to go to jail," I said. "I want to help you. But you'd better start being nice to me. Because this is bad."

"You caused this," he said. "You've just got to run to your friends."

Finally I managed to calm him down, and we got off the phone. But then I had to deal with my friends.

chapter seven

The Polygraph Test

To keep Russell out of jail, I was going to have to convince Mark and Jennifer to drop their charges against him. I felt terrible about how badly Mark had been hurt, and I didn't want to have to ask this of them, but I didn't see any other option. That's when I started realizing just how bad the situation was. I still have so much guilt about this. It was one thing for me to let someone abuse me, but now Russell had really hurt one of my friends, and I had to ask these same friends to cover for him.

At the same time I was protecting Russell, I was more terrified of him than ever. Now that he had gone so far, and was likely to get into trouble, he might decide that things couldn't get any worse and feel free to hurt me more seriously than he had before. And after what I had witnessed, I was more certain than ever that Russell absolutely had the capacity to kill me. I still couldn't believe how much damage Russell had been able to inflict on Mark in those twenty minutes, even while getting hit in the back of the head with a fire log. Not to mention that Russell had thrown three people and a dog into the pool and attempted to drown me.

I was still sure that Russell would never hurt our daughter, but I was worried for my own safety. Before I went home, I confirmed that Russell was still at Rick's house and wasn't planning to come home that day. I also made sure that Gloria was at the house to provide me with a buffer, should Russell decide to surprise me.

I drove home with a heavy heart. It was a relief when I saw that Russell was, in fact, not there. I went inside and tried to act like everything was normal with Kennedy. But I couldn't help but worry about how I would explain it to her if her daddy ended up in prison, in spite of my best efforts. And what it would be like for her to grow up in Beverly Hills with a dad who was locked up. My mind was full of so many fears—from the financial repercussions, to the social stigma—of all that would come with Russell's incarceration. Not to mention my anxiety about how I would take care of Kennedy if Mark sued Russell, and by extension, me. And the guilt I felt about the extent of Mark's injuries and the ferocity of Jennifer's anger.

Later that day, I called Jennifer. She remained furious.

"Mark's going to bury Russell," she said.

Being the conflict-avoidant person I was, having all of this anger directed at me was incredibly uncomfortable. On top of that, I was embarrassed because I knew Russell had behaved like a maniac and that there was no way Jennifer could understand how I could still love him and remain loyal to him. But I did, and I was. Just like I had done since our first date, I had this ability to see the Russell I wanted to believe in—the suave, successful businessman who would protect me from everyone—and deny the behaviors that weren't in keeping with my image of him, even as fewer and fewer people in Russell's life were able to buy into the ideal.

"Everybody looks the other way about how he treats you because you ask us to," she said. "But now you're letting it hurt other people, because you can't get this under control. If you didn't have this person in your life, he would never have been around me or Mark, and then all this never would have happened."

"I know, Jennifer. I'm sorry," I said.

As remorseful as I was, and as nervous as I felt about what Jennifer's reaction would be, I knew that I had to ask her and Mark for a big favor. I gathered my courage.

"I need you not to press charges," I said.

She didn't respond. So I continued.

"I know that everybody is really mad right now, but I don't know how Kennedy and I are going to survive if Russell goes to prison," I said. "He won't be able to earn a living. What's going to happen to Kennedy and me?"

Still she didn't speak.

"Whatever you need for the hospital bills and Mark's dental work, Russell will take care of it," I said.

There was another long pause.

"Please, you don't understand," I said.

"I don't know what we're going to do," she said. "Mark is really hurt. We need to get Mark taken care of and then we'll figure all of this out."

Her words didn't exactly reassure me. As soon as I got off the phone with Jennifer, I called their dentist and told him that whatever it cost to replace Mark's teeth, I'd come by and pay for it. I drove over to his office later that day and paid the $10,000 bill. Then there was nothing to do but wait and see what they would decide. (I later found out that the bill I took care of was the only one: Russell hadn't taken care of Mark's other medical bills.)

In the meantime, I dealt with the fallout at my house. I didn't have any further contact with Russell the day after the fight, but I did check in with our friend Rick several times. Finally, Russell came home that evening. The mood between us was tense. But my reaction to seeing him surprised me. I was afraid of him, but more than anything else, I almost felt sorry for him. As I had seen once again the previous night, it was clear that when Russell was consumed by his extreme anger, he had absolutely no ability to control himself. This seemed sad to me because it was almost like he couldn't help being a bad guy, and yet it brought so much trouble down on him.

I had seen Russell's rages enough times to suspect that there was probably an underlying mental illness behind them, even if I wasn't entirely conscious of my realization back then. But I was very aware that no matter how much I pitied him, I was going to have to be the one to pick up the pieces for this man I loved who couldn't control himself.

"Jennifer is furious," I said.

Russell seemed nervous, which was unusual for him.

"What do you think is going to happen?" he asked.

"I don't know," I said. "I asked her not to press charges, but we'll just have to wait and see."

That's when Russell told me that he had gone to the police station after the attack and filed a police report against Mark. I stared at him in disbelief. It was one thing to think that he was consumed by a rage he couldn't control. It was another thing to realize that he was so calculating that even in all of the chaos of that night, he had been able to gather his thoughts enough to have the idea of protecting himself by pressing charges first. My mind didn't work like that at all, and I understood in that moment that Russell would always be one step ahead of me. He often told me that if I called the police on him, he would drag me through the courts for so long that he would bankrupt me and that he would find a way to take Kennedy away. Of course, looking back, I recognize that it would have been very unlikely for him to gain custody of our daughter instead of me. But back then I believed everything Russell told me, and that was the scariest threat he possibly could have made. Now his actions of the previous night suggested that he was quite capable of carrying out these threats.

In the aftermath of the fight, I received a series of phone calls from the Beverly Hills Police Department. Because Jennifer had told a police officer that Russell had attempted to kill me, they were required to investigate. I avoided the female detective's calls for as long as I could, but finally I knew I had to talk to her. When I did, she expressed grave concern about my safety, but I tried to keep my tone light.

"No, no, he's not going to kill me," I said.

"Well, your friend said he said he was going to kill you," she said.

"No, I'm good, really," I said.

After that, there was nothing to do but wait. It was hard for me to think of anything else for the week or two it took Mark and Jennifer to decide how they were going to proceed. When Jennifer called to tell me their decision, I was incredibly nervous.

"Mark's not going to do anything," she said.

"Thank you, thank you," I said, giddy with relief.

"But the fact that you're living in this situation is ridiculous," she said. "You need to get out of this. He is going to kill you one of these days."

I didn't have anything to say in response to that.

"He is crazy," she said. "He is psychotic. He's not stable. There's something mentally wrong with him."

I didn't have anything to say to that, either.

I was so relieved that they were going to drop the charges. But I knew that the situation would change my relationship with Jennifer. Not only because she could never forgive Russell for what he had done, but also because I knew that she was right. I still wasn't ready to leave, so I didn't want to hear her warnings. With all of my other friends, I could make excuses for Russell's behavior and exaggerate my own responsibility for our fights, but now that Jennifer had seen Russell in action, there was no explaining away his behavior. I think a very small part of me was relieved to finally have someone bear witness to the reality of the violence and chaos I had been living with for the past four years, but at the same time, it was humiliating. And Jennifer was done accepting any excuses for Russell. There was no way she was going to forgive and forget and go to dinner with us, as she had in the past, and as my other friends were still willing to do. And even if she couldn't convince me to leave him, she was not going to allow him to be a part of her life anymore. Jennifer and I didn't speak for a year after that.

At about this time I started to drift out of my therapy, so I didn't have the support of my therapist to turn to, either. But in one of the final sessions we did have, she told me she thought Russell should go to jail.

While that might have been true on some level, it wasn't particularly helpful to me. Soon after that I stopped going to therapy altogether.

Every few months I would get a call from the *Real Housewives* producers. I knew that they were meeting with thousands of women, and it seemed unlikely that I would get cast. But if I did, maybe it would be the opportunity I needed to change my life for the better. I knew that I could not continue to live in this abusive relationship forever, especially as the intensity of Russell's violent outbursts seemed to be worsening over time, but I didn't know how to get out or let go. If I were cast, I figured that having my life on camera would encourage Russell to control his temper and help our relationship.

This may sound delusional, given all I had been through, but my dream was that Russell would change. I still loved him deeply and did not want to live without him. But even if I had to leave, and we ended up getting a divorce, being on the show would mean that I had a job and could take care of my daughter and myself.

At the same time, agreeing to live in front of the cameras was a really big decision, even for those who weren't keeping a secret, as I was. My friend Adrienne Maloof also was being interviewed for the show, and we saw each other often because Kennedy attended preschool with her two sons. After we dropped our kids off at school, Adrienne and I began getting coffee together to talk about the casting process and the show. We spent much of the time discussing the pros and cons of doing the show and the impact it would have on our children. Adrienne was among my close group of friends who knew about the troubles in my marriage, so she also said she thought it would be good for me to do the show because I would have a means of taking care of Kennedy.

Instead of being grateful that I had succeeded in making his problems disappear or feeling like he had gotten lucky and should attempt to better control his temper, Russell continued to behave much as he always had. Throughout that summer and fall, we would have periods of calm when he was consumed with business, and I was busy getting Kennedy ready in the morning, taking her to and from school and play dates with friends, and doing everything I could to make sure she had a happy, fun childhood.

But then, every four to six weeks Russell would erupt over the smallest perceived —or invented—slight or cause for suspicion. And every time Russell verbally attacked me, he went back to four subjects that had obsessed him throughout our relationship: the NBA player, the athlete, the scars he claimed to have seen on my back in Miami, and the scab he actually had seen on my back that winter. No matter how vehemently, or frequently, I denied that I had engaged in sexual relations in regard to any of those situations, Russell simply would not believe me. He began threatening to make me take a polygraph test. The first time he mentioned it, I almost couldn't believe him.

"I'm not taking a polygraph," I said. "I'm not a criminal. That's just ridiculous that you would make your wife take a polygraph."

But he was dead serious. And every time he fought with me after that, he would bring it up and explain his logic about why it made sense.

"Well, if you didn't have anything to hide, you wouldn't feel like you couldn't take one," he said. "If you didn't do any of these things, then I don't know why you care."

As Russell had done in the past, he was finally able to use his powerful skills of persuasion to sell me on the idea. I began to see that there could actually be an advantage to taking a polygraph test. Maybe after the test proved I hadn't done any of the things he had accused me of, he would finally stop belaboring these delusions he'd been obsessed with for years, and I'd never have to hear about them again.

Finally, I agreed to take a polygraph test on November 20, 2009. I expected to approach the day with a feeling of relief, only I hadn't counted on how humiliating it would be. The person who was examined right before me had been accused of shoplifting and had a police escort.

The other problem was that as soon as I walked into the room and found myself being hooked up to this foreboding-looking electric machine by a complete stranger, I began to feel like a criminal, even though I knew I had done absolutely nothing wrong. And then I started to get nervous. By this point in my marriage, my anxiety was already incredibly high, even on a good day, and this was real cause for stress.

What if I fail? I thought. *My marriage will be over, and he'll forever think I'm a bad person.*

I didn't really understand how the machine worked, but I had an idea that it monitored my pulse and blood pressure, and my heart was pounding. The fact that Russell was standing in the corner staring at me wasn't helping, either. I was afraid the test would pick up my anxiety and turn it into an indication of deception and guilt where there was none.

I looked to the examiner for reassurance.

"My heart is pounding," I said. "I'm so nervous. Is that going to affect the test?"

He explained that the machine picked up fluctuations in heart rate, so if I remained equally nervous throughout the test, it would know that I wasn't lying. I didn't feel particularly reassured.

He asked me the four questions that Russell wanted answers to:

Had I ever had any kind of sex with the NBA player?

"No."

Had I had any kind of sex with the athlete?

"No."

Was the scab on my lower back caused by something sexual?

"No."

During the course of our marriage, had I ever had any kind of sex with anyone besides Russell Armstrong?

"No."

I was so humiliated to have this man I didn't know ask me these questions that basically suggested I was a liar, and a cheat, and a whore who liked rough sex. I could barely look him in the eye throughout the duration of the examination, and when I glanced over at Russell, I felt even more anxious, so I kept my eyes down.

The test indicated that there had been no deception during the polygraph examination. Then a computer was used to analyze the test results, and I was given an autoscore that again determined that no deception was indicated. Russell had the results additionally reviewed by a second polygraph examiner, who agreed that I had told the truth.

I was relieved, but when I left the office, I felt humiliated and filthy. And of course Russell never apologized for his false accusations. The most I got out of him was this:

"Thank you for doing that for me," he said.

But even then there was almost the implication that it had been a reasonable request all along. Things were peaceful for a short time, and I was grateful for the reprieve from being grilled on those four subjects.

And then, within the next month, Russell started in on me about something or other, and he brought up a new accusation:

"You faked the polygraph," he said.

"What?" I said.

"You paid off the examiner," he said. "Or you knew how to trick a polygraph machine."

I felt deflated. I realized there would be nothing further I could do to make him see the truth. He had something in his mind that wouldn't allow him to let go of his delusions, and it was breaking my heart.

And then, in every fight we had after that, he was on me again about how that scab on my back had been from sex with someone else. He truly believed I was lying about that right up until the end.

My relationship with Russell had reached a plateau of bad. There didn't seem to be a solution in sight. I knew by this point that I certainly didn't have the strength to just wake up one day and leave him. Something needed to happen, bad or good, to make me leave. Luckily, the next something that happened was good. After ten months of waiting and hoping, I got the call telling me that I had been chosen as one of the six cast members for *The Real Housewives of Beverly Hills*.

When I first told Russell the news, he didn't want me to do the show. But then he changed his mind a few days later and gave me his permission. I know it's hard to believe that someone with as many secrets as Russell had, which I didn't even begin to know the extent of at the time, would agree to appear on a reality show. I think his decision to do the show speaks to his extreme narcissism. He thought that everyone loved him, and he would often come home from business meetings and say, "I met with this guy today, he thinks I'm the greatest." And so I believe that he thought this would simply be an even greater platform for even more people to love him. I think he truly believed that he could fool the cameras like he fooled everyone else in his life, including me.

I had no idea what to expect, but I was really excited to be doing the show. And when I learned who my castmates were, I was even more certain that I was about to embark on an amazing experience. As I've already mentioned, I was friends with Adrienne before the show started. And through her, I knew of Lisa, who is—of course—her neighbor across the street. My good friend Linda Thompson was friends with Kelsey and Camille, and I was looking forward to getting to know Camille as well. I had previously met Kyle at a party, and we also had a mutual friend in common, and then, of course, Kim is Kyle's sister, so we were all just one or two degrees of separation away from each other's lives before the show started. I felt very positive about having all of these women begin to play an even greater role in my life.

And then, in March 2010, the cameras started rolling. And they were on us, pretty much constantly, until that October. Obviously it wasn't possible for them to broadcast all of the footage they shot; there's just too much to cram into one season. They could not represent every aspect of our lives, or reveal them in their entirety, but I do think the show captured the overall essence of who we each are as individuals and what our lives were like as a collective during that year.

At the same time, I felt more inhibited than I had expected when I found myself faced with the cameras for the first time. And I think it was a combination of my underlying insecurities and my desire to keep a certain side of my life secret that caused me to play up the aspects of my personality and life that I thought viewers would be expecting from a typical Beverly Hills housewife. It was simply a manifestation of the same problems that had always plagued me. I've honestly come to believe that reality TV does nothing more than amplify who we are, both good and bad.

Of course, it was hard for me to know who I was by that point, because I had already changed so much in my efforts to stay one step ahead of Russell's anger. It had reached the point where my longtime friends had begun commenting on how different I was.

When Russell and I first met, I used to smile constantly. I'm sure my need to be perpetually pleasant and cheerful was partly a manifestation of my people-pleasing behavior. But I also had a genuine tendency to be extremely emotive with people I cared about. If I happened to run into a good friend, such as Linda Thompson, in a restaurant, my immediate reaction was to laugh, squeal, and run over and give her the biggest hug while telling her how happy I was to see her. Whenever Russell witnessed this type of behavior, he would glower from across the room. When I rejoined him, still smiling from the pleasure of seeing my dear friend, he would mock me by smiling at me in the most obnoxious way possible, until my smile died on my face.

"You look like an idiot when you do that," he would say. "You look like the dumb blonde that people think you are. And when you squeal when you run up to your friends, you sound like a high school girl. It's humiliating for me."

"I'm sorry," I would say, not even wanting to smile anymore.

The next time I saw Linda, I would start to react in my usual way, and then I would feel Russell's eyes on me.

After enough of these unpleasant scenes with Russell, I had found myself not smiling as much and greeting even my closest friends with a subdued hello. I began modifying my behavior in all social situations. But because Russell always found something to criticize, it was nearly impossible to please him. If I were too nice to his clients, he would say I was flirting with them. If I weren't nice enough, because I was afraid he would accuse me of flirting, he would say I had been rude to them.

After four years of Russell's constant corrections, I felt like a Stepford Wife. It was impossible for me to relax in social situations when Russell was around because I was monitoring every single aspect of my behavior to avoid setting him off.

But I could never come up with the right formula, and there were many nights when he punished me by beating my head against the car door after we left an event or party, even after we had started filming the show. People began telling me it was like I was two different people, depending on whether Russell was there. And his behavior toward me was beginning to take its toll, even when he wasn't present.

My anxiety level was so high all the time that I had trouble gaining weight. Even though Russell often told me that I was so skinny it was disgusting, and made me change my clothes if he thought an outfit made me look too thin, and even though I ate, my system was under so much stress all the time that I couldn't seem to do anything about it. Sometimes I couldn't eat because I had no appetite. My heart was always racing. My stomach was always in knots. But even when I did eat, my body couldn't seem to recover.

From the beginning, Russell found that his plan to win people over through the show wasn't going to be quite as easy as he had thought. He never felt comfortable in front of the cameras, and because of this, so much of his personality didn't come across on the show.

Russell never lost his temper on-camera. But by this point in our marriage, he didn't have to for people in Beverly Hills to know about the abuse. There had been enough public incidents, and people had seen me cry enough times to know that there was at least verbal abuse in our marriage. Beverly Hills is a small neighborhood, and people talk. I began to realize that people were aware of the problems in my marriage, even without the cameras focused on us.

"We've all seen you leave charity events crying, or seen you crying at events," a friend said to me at one point.

When I thought about this, I knew it was true. Russell so frequently spoke unkindly to me when we were out, and I was so terrified of what he was going to do to me after these events, that it was impossible for me to hide my emotions, as much as I tried.

chapter eight

"I've Got to Get Out
of This Relationship"

One night, Russell started screaming at me at an event. He then stormed off and left me without a ride home, as he had done so many times before. Only, something *had* changed. In the past, it had been difficult for me to maintain close friendships, both because of my discomfort with intimacy, and later, my desire to protect Russell from my friends' judgment about the way he treated me. But the nature of the show meant that my castmates and I were forced to be intimate with each other, day in and day out, for seven months at a time. No matter how uncomfortable I sometimes felt being so close to them, I could only retreat from them so far. Ultimately I think this was very healthy for me, especially because I was at a point in my marriage when I was trying to gain the courage and strength I needed to finally make Russell get help and change his behavior, or to leave him once and for all. I have spoken with the other girls on the show about how we are almost like sisters, and how much we always held each other accountable for our behavior. I think this took me out of my comfort zone in a really healthy way.

Having five strong personalities around me made me grow stronger. It made me realize that I didn't need to be a people-pleaser to please people. I finally understood that standing up for myself and speaking my mind in the moment was how I was going to teach people how I wanted to be treated. Seeing how my five castmates lived their lives made me see more clearly than ever before how much I wanted to change myself—but in a positive, healing way, this time—and my life. The realization gave me hope that I could grow stronger, find my voice, and finally achieve equality in my marriage.

The show was a big catalyst for me to take a more honest look at my relationship with Russell, not only because it was about to be in the public eye, but also because I was interacting with other married women and seeing what their relationships were like. Once I sized up my marriage in comparison, I had to admit all that was wrong with it and finally try to do something about the problems. Not that this all happened right away. At first the changes were small.

On the night when Russell left me at yet another event, instead of going home and facing more of his abuse, or crawling into bed with my daughter to hide from him, I took a cab to Lisa's restaurant, Sur. She was having dinner there with Kyle, and when I walked into the restaurant and joined them at their table, I was bawling. The show's producers were sitting at another table in the restaurant. There was no hiding how upset I was.

These moments began to add up. They gave me some

much-needed perspective and made Russell begin to feel like his actions could have consequences. One night, I was out at an event with Lisa, and I received a text message from Russell:

"Fuck you, you whore."

I started to tear up.

"What's wrong?" she asked.

I tried to shake off her question, but she was too concerned about me to drop her inquiries. She looked at my BlackBerry, and when she saw what Russell had written, she became very upset.

"That's unacceptable," she said, her tone laced with disgust.

I had never thought about it that way before. I cried harder.

"You've got to get out of this," she said. "Because every time I see you, you're crying. You're losing too much weight. You're clearly not handling this situation well."

After that, Lisa's behavior toward Russell cooled significantly, and he was very aware of this shift and immediately suspected why it had occurred.

Another time, I was at Lisa's house for a photo shoot for the show. During a moment when just the two of us were talking, I asked her about something I had always taken for granted.

"Does your husband ever check your phone?" I asked.

"I would leave my husband if he went through my phone," she said.

"Oh, really?" I asked, genuinely surprised.

She and her husband had been married for nearly thirty years, so obviously they were doing something right. I figured they probably knew everything about each other's lives and phone books anyhow, so I didn't understand why she would care. And then it hit me that her response wasn't about the information in her phone itself; it was about the fact that checking her phone was disrespectful. She wouldn't have tolerated such treatment.

At the same time that the show was bringing to light the abuse I'd been living with for so long, it gave me the opportunity to publically champion the work of the 1736 Family Crisis Center, where I continued to volunteer. During the first season, I hosted a charity poker tournament featuring Annie Duke for the center. Partway through the event, I spoke out about my own childhood experiences in hopes that people would start to see that domestic violence affects people from all walks of life. As I stood there, holding the microphone in my hand and staring out at the sea of faces, including my cast-mates, who had become such good friends, the enormity of all I had been through and continued to experience began to press down on me. My lips quivered, and I began to cry. I don't know if anyone in the audience that night recognized it, but I wasn't just upset by the childhood memories I was revealing. The pressure of trying to stay one step ahead of Russell's abuse while trying to keep his behavior a secret from others was beginning to become more than I could bear.

And then, on October 14, 2010, the show began to air and the eyes of the world were upon us. When the first episodes ran, I immediately felt uncomfortable with how I appeared in front of the cameras. I don't think I had realized until that moment how much I had been changed by my marriage and how much my desire to come across as the stereotypical,

Botoxed, and status-obsessed Beverly Hills housewife had led me to misrepresent my personality during that first season.

When I watched the first season, I saw my Stepford Wife behavior. I saw the obvious differences between my relationship and that of Kyle and Mauricio or Ken and Lisa. I witnessed my inability to stand my ground and speak up for myself. I saw it all, and at times I hated myself as much as some of the hostile people on Twitter did.

There was one upside to all of this, though. I knew that Russell also could see the differences in our marriage in contrast to the others on the show, and I had high hopes that this was going to be a revelation for him, too. I knew he loved me, and I hoped he would be motivated to work on our relationship and control his rage. I wanted most to repair the damage and heal the scars; even after everything, I loved him very much, and still do. I wanted this healing for us; but more than anything, I wanted it for Kennedy. I wanted her to have both of us, together and happily married, forever.

I began reading the press that surrounded the show and the comments posted on the Internet. This was painful for me because I realized that I was coming across as superficial, and that it was my own fault because I hadn't had the confidence to think that people could like the person I really was. Of course, looking back I can see that I was actually cast because of this other, real, side. The producers had wanted to show the diversity of women in Beverly Hills, and the fact that not all of them had come from money, and that some of them had struggled.

One of the hardest aspects of the press coverage for me was the scrutiny and ridicule I received regarding my plastic surgery. For one thing, I've had much less work done than most people assume. Other than some Botox and other fillers and injections, the only significant work I've had done is my lip implant and breast augmentation. Yes, those cheekbones are mine; I'm part Cherokee Indian, and those are the cheeks I've always had. And I can't imagine anyone being thrilled about having their high school pictures unearthed. But I soon found a way to laugh about the situation. As I started to joke, the aspect of those pictures I find most embarrassing is how big my hair was in high school. I've even teased my mom about how she let me walk around like that.

"Did you not love me?" I would say.

And then I made peace with all of it. I decided, once and for all, that I would not remove my lip implant, and that people would just have to continue making their Daffy Duck jokes. That, I could handle. Compared to everything else I've been through, the question of how I look and how people feel about it seems insignificant to me.

At the time I also found it upsetting that the press tried to make something out of nothing, particularly the matter of my multiple name changes. I've always been very open about when and why I changed my name, and it bothered me that they tried to suggest I was running away from something unsavory in my past. As I've said again and again, the only thing I was trying to escape was my own insecurities and painful associations from my childhood.

It didn't take me long to stop reading any of it. I've always felt that it's just as dangerous to buy into the nice things that people say in the press and on the blogs, because it creates the temptation to buy into the negative things, too. So I chose not to read either side. When reports cross my path now, I do my best not to let them bother me.

Russell, on the other hand, was instantly obsessed with any and all responses to the show, both in the press and the public realm. He was quick to believe the good. And anything negative that was written about either of us was enough to consume his thoughts completely.

When the show first began to air, Russell signed up for Google Alerts so that he received a notification when anything appeared on the Internet about him or about me. The first items to surface involved two men who claimed they had dated me in high school. Of course, this was the worst possible trigger for Russell's jealousy, and he grilled me incessantly about both men and our past romantic histories. It didn't matter that, as I told him again and again, I hadn't dated one of the men at all. And I had only gone to a prom with the other guy because he was friends with my boyfriend, who was away at college at the time. Russell would not believe me, or be placated, and he turned the conversations into fights.

Of course, the one guy I really did date for years in high school sent me an e-mail through my publicist telling me that the tabloids were bombarding him with requests for interviews about me. When he told them that he didn't have anything but nice things to say about me, they no longer wanted an interview.

And then a Google Alert came in about Russell. I think there was a small part of him that enjoyed the attention because the fact that people were talking about him made him feel important. But that didn't last for long. The first story to come out in the press had to do with Russell's bankruptcy. He was embarrassed that the truth of his troubled financial past had surfaced, and he worried that it would hurt his ability to attract clients to his venture capital firm. But the only emotion he openly expressed was anger, and it made it even more impossible than ever to live with him.

When I opened my eyes every morning, the first thing I saw was Russell on his BlackBerry in bed next to me, frantically reading whatever was coming in on Google Alert. This became a major source of stress because every day without fail there was something new in the press about me, or him, or both of us. It was rarely positive.

"Please get off Google," I repeatedly said to him.

He tried to suggest that he had a good reason for reading the stories.

"I need to know what's being said about me out there so I know what to expect for my business," he said.

But this wasn't just good business practice; he was hooked. And as the show's popularity took off, there were sometimes as many as twenty different stories about us on Google Alert on any given day. The stories poisoned his mood, even when they were completely false. And when Russell was in a bad mood, everything was bad for everyone around him for the rest of that day. Any little thing that went wrong would set him off. If Kennedy was grouchy while I dressed her for school, he took it out on me.

"Oh, you're just a great mother!" he would say. "You didn't

get her to bed on time, and she didn't get enough sleep last night, and now she's fussy."

Even more frequently, he would go through the entire morning in moody silence. And then, when I was upstairs working in our office or helping Kennedy get ready for school, I would hear the front door slam behind him as he left for work without saying a word to me. Even though I knew he was actually upset at whatever he had read on Google Alert that morning—not at me—I would spend the rest of the day living with the anxiety of the fact that I knew he was mad, but I didn't know about what, and that there was the chance that he would take it out on me when I finally saw him later. When I look back, I really regret the productivity I lost for all of those years because I was so focused on keeping him happy that I couldn't get anything else done.

I wasn't the only one to notice that Russell's fixation on Google Alert had become a problem. He spent all day on Google, and even people at his office were aware of how it was affecting him. They told me that his obsession with Google Alert was consuming him.

Next door to Russell's office was a PR firm run by two women who did some work for him. He began spending hours in their office, ranting about whatever was on Google Alert that day. During a phone conversation with one of these women, I brought up his Google addiction. We joked that we should make him a T-shirt with a no-smoking logo, but instead of the cigarette, the red line would cross out the word "Google."

There was no reasoning with Russell, and it soon became

clear that the media scrutiny was eating away at him, especially as more of his skeletons began to come to light throughout the first season. Of course, at the time I didn't know just how much Russell was hiding, and how much anxiety he must have been feeling as he worried about what would surface next and how bad the fallout would be.

I wasn't surprised when the stories about Russell's bankruptcy surfaced because, of course, I knew about that. But then the press delivered some unpleasant shocks. Reports surfaced about past litigation Russell had faced, a past securities fraud charge, and his prosecution for tax evasion, including the penalty he had paid and the 150 hours of community service he had completed. Next out was the story about his arrest for domestic violence when he was married to his first wife. I knew that Russell had been ordered to undergo two years of anger management courses because of a fight between him and his ex, but he had told me that the entire thing had been a misunderstanding, and that she had attacked him, and he had only been defending himself. Once her court testimony was all over the Internet, it became evident that the truth was much closer to the kind of abuse I had experienced during our marriage. Also included in that story was a statement from a former girlfriend who had a less violent, but similar, tale to tell. I was horrified to realize that my husband had a long history of domestic violence.

Russell, on the other hand, was more disturbed by the bad press about his financial dealings. Because his business involved investing money for his clients, he was mortified that people would think he was anything less than completely honest, or feel like he wasn't qualified to handle their money because he couldn't manage his own. He worried obsessively about how this might affect his business. Frankly, so did I.

At one point Russell confessed that prospective clients were beginning to ask him about these negative news stories before entering into deals with him. It wasn't long before he felt like the bad publicity surrounding the show was having a detrimental affect on his ability to make money. As the image he had so carefully constructed began to unravel, so did Russell. He was deeply concerned about what people, especially his children, thought about him, and when the public perception became increasingly negative, it frustrated him.

Russell had thought that he would be able to control the whole world as completely as he controlled me, but by the end of the first season, this was clearly not the case. As the pressures mounted, he became increasingly volatile and difficult to live with. Fortunately, I soon had an ally in my home.

In January 2011, I hired my high school cheerleading coach's daughter Julie as a personal assistant. She moved into our Bel Air home so I could keep an eye on her for her mother, and she could more easily do her job for me. It didn't take long for her to witness Russell's explosive rage, but he tried to put a spin on the situation like he always did. After Russell had screamed at me in our bedroom at night, he would go down to Julie's bedroom in the morning and knock on her door.

"I'm sorry I got so upset last night, and I'm sorry you had to hear all that," he would say.

Julie always acted like it wasn't a big deal, but I think she was taking stock of the situation, and her loyalties were clearly with me. As I later learned, when she heard Russell and me come in at night, she would stay awake, listening for the sound of a fight. If she heard Russell screaming at me, she would come out of her room and wait in the kitchen, or at the bottom of the stairs, until she heard my voice and knew that I wasn't hurt. Sometimes, when things sounded particularly bad, she sent our dog, Jax, upstairs so that she could come upstairs after him. While she was apologizing to us for letting Jax get away from her, she would really be checking on me to make sure I was okay. I definitely felt safer having Julie in the house. Because she was like family, I knew I could trust her not to tell anyone about Russell's outbursts, and I didn't think that Russell would hurt me if she were there to witness it.

Unfortunately, as I would soon learn, Russell's moods were becoming so volatile that he was not able to control his violent temper, even when potential witnesses were nearby. At the end of January, we traveled to Dallas for the Super Bowl and stayed with one of Russell's oldest friends, and his wife and family, in the suburb of Highland Park.

I had several appearances scheduled before the game, including a stop at a gifting suite, where a large group of people gathered around me, asking if they could take one-on-one pictures with me. And then, when we arrived at the Dallas Cowboys Stadium, people kept stopping me for pictures. I could tell that Russell was getting agitated. He always seemed fine if people wanted their picture taken with both of us, but if they only wanted a picture with me, it clearly bothered him. I was keeping an eye on Russell, and I could see his mood darkening. But while I was trying to keep him happy, I didn't want to be rude to fans of the show who wanted to take pictures. I could tell he was becoming increasingly impatient and really just wanted to watch the game. Then a woman approached me with a gift. It was just too much for him.

"I'm going to go sit down," he snapped. "You can find your own way back to your seat."

I watched him nervously as he stalked off, and I tried to end my conversation with the woman as quickly as possible so I could join him at our seats. Finally things settled down, and we had a good enough time at the game despite his irritation, so I assumed everything was fine.

From there we went to a Mexican restaurant in Highland Park for margaritas and food with some of Russell's old friends from Texas. When we got to the restaurant, the hostess took us straight upstairs to a smaller, more private dining area. We were with a big group of people and wanted to sit where our group could talk without interruption.

After we got settled at the table and ordered our drinks, three young women bounced up to our table. They were fans of the show, and they wanted a picture with me. I agreed and stood up to pose with them. They had all been drinking, so they were having a great time and being loud and boisterous. Russell had gone to the restroom, and when he returned, I was posing with the girls. They must have been hanging on me more than Russell liked.

I began to get anxious as I saw Russell glowering at me, and I tried to wrap up our conversation. But the girls were drunk and excited, and they kept giggling and chatting. Finally, I hugged them all as they thanked me for the picture, and they went back to their seats.

Before I could sit down at our table, Russell grabbed me by my arm, yanked me over to a service door, and pushed me inside. We were at the top of a staircase the staff used to go back and forth to the kitchen. He was really furious by this point, and as soon as the door closed, he hit me twice in the jaw with the butt of his open hand.

"You're embarrassing me!" he screamed. "You're embarrassing my friends! And you're being fucking rude to my friends!"

I started to cry and ran down the back service stairs so I could go to the bathroom and compose myself. When I had calmed down, I went up the front staircase and rejoined our group. As I sat down, a woman at a nearby table caught my eye. I could tell that she recognized me from the show and that she could tell I'd been crying.

"Are you okay?" she asked.

I nodded and tried to smile at her, but she wasn't fooled.

"I know what's going on," she said.

"No, no, no, I'm okay," I said.

We talked for a couple of minutes, and while we did, I could tell that Russell was watching everything I did to make sure I didn't make any confessions. She knew several of the people at our table, and she was as sweet as could be. In fact, she insisted on giving me her number.

"If you ever need anything, call me," she said.

When we got back Russell's friends' house, I could tell that Russell had not calmed down at all, and I didn't want to be

near him. His friends' daughte

in her bedroom talking to one ol

there with her. Russell's friend's w

were sitting together, talking. I was up,

pened at the restaurant and scared abo,

next, and I kept tearing up as I told them a,

"We've got a lot of problems, and he gets p,
I said.

Russell came to the door and saw me with tears
He was furious.

"Oh, here she goes again, she's going to cry to everyon
sneered, and then he stalked away.

I stayed in the daughter's bedroom for about an hour, hop
ing that Russell would go to sleep. But he finally came in to
get me.

"Taylor, you need to come to bed now," he said.

My heart racing, I looked around for an escape, but I knew
there was none, so I got up and went with him. I felt a certain
level of protection because we were in someone else's house,
but I could tell that his mood was very dark, and that made
me anxious.

When Russell shut the door to the guest room behind us, I
hurried into the bathroom and started getting ready for bed. He
came flying into the bathroom, spun me around, and started
hitting me in the jaw. After several blows, something snapped.
The pain was excruciating, and I could no longer shut my
mouth. Russell had knocked my jaw out of the socket. He kept
hitting me.

I put both my hands up to shield my face and fell to the

ver the toilet. I still couldn't close my mouth, and saliva
unning down into the toilet bowl.

*Oh, my God, I'm going to have to call an ambulance because
n't shut my mouth,* I thought. *This time I'm really hurt.*

Instead of getting mad at Russell for injuring me so severely,
instantly began to worry that when the ambulance came, they
would make me file a police report, which I didn't want to do.

I'm going to have to tell on him, I thought. *Oh, my God, I
don't want him to go to jail.*

Even when he had been so violent and cruel, I was more
concerned about protecting him than about my own well-
being.

I kneeled over the toilet, trying to figure out how to get my
mouth closed so I wouldn't have to go to the hospital.

"You're overreacting, as usual," he said.

I ignored him and tried to wiggle my jaw. He leaned over me.

"Oh, go run and tell everyone," he said. "Go call all your
friends. Tell everyone that I hit you again. Go make a big deal
out of this."

"I'm really hurt," I said slowly, talking as best as I could
while holding my jaw still and moving only my tongue. "I need
some help."

"Do you want me to call an ambulance?" he taunted me.
"Do you want me to call an ambulance so you can make a big
scene out of this?"

Finally I got myself up off the floor and lay down in bed on
my back. I still couldn't close my mouth. I stared at the ceiling
and tried to ignore the pain.

I know I need to see a doctor right now, I thought.

But I was too scared to go because I didn't want Russell to go to jail. And I was embarrassed, too, because we were at his friends' house and they had a really strong marriage. Finally, I was able to pop my jaw back into place, but I was still in terrible pain. Russell lay down next to me.

"Just relax," he said quietly. "You'll feel better in the morning."

I had to sleep on my back that night, and for the next two nights, and eat really carefully, but I never did see a doctor for that injury. I thought it had healed itself, but I still get shooting nerve pain in my jaw from time to time when I'm eating, which always reminds me of that night and makes me very sad.

Of course, even after we got home, Russell was still angry at me for talking with his friend's wife about our problems, and he continued to blame me for how the evening had ended.

"I'm done," he said. "I'm out of here. We're done. I'm moving. Tomorrow morning there's going to be a moving company here, and I'm leaving."

In the past, when Russell had threatened to leave, I had begged him to stay. But the severity of the injury to my jaw had changed things for me. The violence of the attack and the fact that it had happened with other people around had scared me. I may not have wanted Russell to go to jail, but I definitely did not want to live like that anymore.

I've got to get out of this relationship because he went way too far, I thought.

When Russell told me he was moving out, I agreed that it was for the best, and he started looking online for places to live. He printed out the listings for several high-rises that had vacancies and said he had hired a moving company and was leaving the next day. I had previously made plans to have lunch with Camille in Malibu that day. Kennedy was with her grandparents, and I decided that a trip to Malibu would be a good escape.

When Camille and I met at Taverna Tony for lunch, I shared with her the latest development in the ongoing saga of my marriage.

"Russell's moving out tomorrow," I said.

"Are you okay?" she asked.

"I think I am finally okay with it," I said. "Things have just gotten so bad."

When I told Camille about what had happened following the Super Bowl, she was horrified. I had told her about Russell in the past, but she could tell that something was different now. Before when it had been suggested that I should leave Russell, she had been honest about the fact that she didn't think I was ready and reminded me of what her divorce attorney had said to her when she had first entered his office:

"If you're really ready to do this, then let's do this, but if you're not, then you should turn around and walk out of here, because there's no gray area with this stuff."

But now she leaned back in her chair and appraised me closely.

"You actually seem ready," she said.

"I think I am," I said. "Can you give me some advice?"

I knew that she had gone through the challenges of a high-profile divorce while trying to minimize the impact on her young children.

"How do I tell Kennedy?" I asked. "Do I tell her now? Do I let Russell move out first?"

Our lunch lasted for a few hours, and Camille was incredibly supportive and reassuring about Kennedy. There was just one problem. As resolved as I seemed on the outside, and as much as I had tried to convince myself otherwise, I *really* didn't want Russell to move out, even after everything he had just put me through. I know it's hard for people who haven't experienced abuse to understand, but even with how he had degraded me and hurt me emotionally and physically, I still didn't want to live without him. I still loved him, and even more than that, I had become addicted to the cycle of violence in which we had lived for so long.

Apparently Russell was still caught up in our pattern, too. When I returned to the house that evening, he wasn't there. But instead of moving out, he had gone to the office, and he came home later that night. When he didn't leave the following day, I didn't confront him about his change of plans, and we didn't talk about what had happened to make him decide to stay. The day of his supposed departure came and went; no moving truck, no drama. I was relieved that I hadn't lost him after all, but I was finally convinced that something had to change in our marriage, once and for all.

chapter nine

"It's Your Fault"

I had always been able to partly justify my inability to leave our abusive marriage with the fact that Russell had never exhibited the worst of his anger in front of Kennedy. I still thought it was better for her to live with an imperfect father than no father at all. I know that some people might have difficulty believing that I truly did not think Kennedy was in danger—and of course now I can recognize that the emotional danger I put her in was significant—but I did my best to protect her.

We still had our live-in nanny, Gloria, who slept in Kennedy's room five nights a week, so I always knew there was someone with her if things got ugly between Russell and me. And I had seen Russell be very cautious about never harming me—or even yelling at me—in front of Kennedy or the boys. While I later found out that Russell's first wife had stated in a court filing that someone had seen Russell slap his son, I had never seen anything like that with any of the children, and if I had, I wouldn't have stood for it. I may not have thought I deserved to be treated well, but I knew that they did. I felt strongly that the abuse was about me; it wasn't about them. Russell loved his children and was good to them.

But that winter, Kennedy, who was just turning five at the time, began to exhibit signs that the abuse was starting to affect her after all. When Russell and I were talking alone in the office, or the bedroom, she would come in and sit on my lap or stand in the room with her arms crossed, staring at us, and she refused to leave us alone. It got to the point where we couldn't talk about any serious topics because she was always there watching over our conversations. It was as if she considered it her responsibility to protect me from her father. I thought back to how I had pulled my dad's hair to get him to stop hitting my mom and vowed that I would do what was right for my daughter.

A few days later I finally found a moment to talk to Russell alone.

"Listen, I'm exhausted and something has to change," I said, teary-eyed. "Things are out of control, and we're falling apart. I really got hurt last time, and it could have been worse. I could have had a broken jaw."

What I didn't go on to say, but I feel like we both were thinking—I know it's what *I* was thinking—was how long a broken jaw takes to heal, and how, if he had broken my jaw, I would have gone into filming season two of the show with my jaw wired shut. That would have required some serious explaining.

Russell seemed to recognize that he had lost control in Texas, even for him, and I think the experience was almost as scary for him as it was for me. Something had definitely changed within him because he finally agreed to accompany me to couples' therapy.

As it is for many couples, therapy was a last-ditch effort for us to save a relationship that had been in trouble from the very beginning. I had mixed feelings about how much good it was really going to do. Yes, Russell and I had finally acknowledged that we either needed to get help, or get away from each other, because it wasn't safe for our life together to continue as it was. But I feared that he would try to manipulate our therapist, just as he was able to do with everyone else in his life. When we had our first meeting with Dr. Charlie Sophy, whom Adrienne referred me to, my fears seemed justified. During our first session, Dr. Sophy asked us each to identify the source of our tensions. I was too afraid to speak my mind at that point, but luckily, Dr. Sophy sensed the reason for my silence right away. Meanwhile, as usual, Russell blamed everything on me.

"Well, she didn't call me when she was supposed to," Russell said. "And she was supposed to be home at eleven-thirty, but she wasn't home until twelve-thirty."

Russell was good at justifying his position. And he was so persuasive as he spoke that Dr. Sophy seemed convinced, at least for a while. It took even our incredibly intelligent, very experienced therapist a couple of sessions to see through Russell. By about the third session, though, Dr. Sophy got clear on what was really happening in our marriage. He recognized the significance of my body language and posture in relationship to Russell; how I would move back in my seat and bow my head slightly at times when I was afraid to talk. When

Dr. Sophy asked for my opinion, he could see that I didn't feel safe giving it. Without witnessing any actual verbal or physical abuse, he saw everything. Soon he stepped in and the therapy really began.

Almost immediately, Dr. Sophy could assess that we had real problems. I hadn't found the courage to tell him about my jaw yet, and he didn't know about a lot of the painful things that had transpired over the years. But what he did know was that we were not in a healthy, happy marriage built on mutual respect and equality. That was obvious.

In addition to our weekly couples' therapy sessions, I began attending private sessions with Dr. Sophy. My objective was to find my voice: to find the courage to speak up for myself in the moment without fear of rejection; to learn to respect myself by asking others to do the same. I also wanted to finally let go of my shame, and to break the cycle of violence, for good.

Russell and I frequently spoke with Dr. Sophy on the phone as well. The rules of our treatment included a commitment to call Dr. Sophy the moment when tensions started to rise. If we were both home I would go into one room and Russell would go into another, and we would each have our turn to talk while Dr. Sophy mediated. Our other commitment was that we would talk only about our marital problems within the confines of therapy. No more running to my friends for advice; I now had to confront it head-on, with Russell, face-to-face. Dr. Sophy held each of us accountable for speaking the truth, and that meant I was going to have to get a backbone, and fast. He texted both of us frequently to check in throughout the day, and still does this for me to this day, little notes that read:

"U ok?" or "All ok?" Dr. Sophy was bound and determined to help us, by saving our marriage, or by having us accept that it was time to walk away.

Shortly after we started treatment, Dr. Sophy recommended that Russell go on medication. I was all for the idea, because I was hoping that it could keep Russell's anger in check. But I knew that Russell would be a hard sell. He was very adverse to medication because he felt like his mother's personality had been dimmed by the psychiatric medication she was on, and he didn't want that to happen to him.

While Russell was candid about why he didn't want to be medicated, he never opened up to me about what he felt his mental state was really like during this time. Looking back, I don't think he really knew. But I see now that it must have been much darker than he let on during our day-to-day life together, especially given what happened later.

On March 16, 2011, Russell began taking medication. I was thrilled that he was approaching our therapy and his treatment so seriously. My plan was to keep him calm and keep Dr. Sophy on speed dial until the magical pills began to transform the angry man I loved. This could be our saving grace and our ticket to happiness, I thought. Finally I had gotten Russell into therapy, and now he was going to feel and act more calmly, thanks to the help of his medication. But Dr. Sophy cautioned us that it would take several weeks for the medication to have any noticeable affect on Russell or his behavior.

Russell took his first pill at 8:00 a.m., and by noon the medication had already kicked in. Right away he kept telling me how different he felt.

"This is amazing," he said. "I feel like nothing could bother me today."

What? I thought. *Dr. Sophy said this was going to take a few weeks to start working. How is that possible? Did we just discover our miracle?*

I couldn't believe it. When I later discussed with Dr. Sophy how quickly the meds had worked, he explained to me that when this occurs in patients, it is typically a sign that the chemical imbalances in their brains are quite severe. This was hard for me to hear. As much as it excited me that Russell was feeling better so quickly, the ramifications of what the speediness of his transformation might mean scared the hell out of me as well.

Although it was a relief to see such a marked improvement in Russell's overall mood and stability, I had been living with the terrifying fallout from his psychological problems for too long to let my guard down so easily. The peace seemed tenuous, since I knew that his anger was only being controlled by his medication. I wanted to commit to staying and working through it all, to letting the past go, to forgiving and forgetting. But my anxious self had fears that couldn't be quieted just like that.

What happens if he misses a dose? What happens if he decides to stop taking the medication altogether and goes into a rage?

These worries created another source of anxiety for me as I tried to make sure Russell was taking his pills without letting him know I was doing so.

"I'm going downstairs to get our coffee," I would say. "Don't forget to take your medicine, honey."

Or

"Have a great day at the office, sweetie," I would say. "Did you take your medicine?"

Now I was mothering my husband, but I didn't know what else to do.

As we continued on our treatment path, the medication definitely seemed to make a huge difference. We still had a great deal to work through, but without Russell's anger flaring up, our issues were minimized.

After several sessions, Dr. Sophy diagnosed me with PTSD. When he first said my diagnosis, I couldn't believe it.

There must be another PTSD than post-traumatic stress disorder, I thought. *I have only heard of war veterans who have served on the front lines and seen the horrors of battle being diagnosed with PTSD. I am a Beverly Hills housewife, not a soldier. I can't have PTSD.*

Well, I was wrong. Housewives can get PTSD, too, and yours, truly did. Dr. Sophy urged me to look up the diagnosis and learn more about it.

"The person has experienced, witnessed, or been confronted with an event or events that involve actual or threatened death or serious injury, or a threat to the physical integrity of oneself or others."

Check.

"The person's response involved intense fear, helplessness, or horror."

Check.

Dr. Sophy prescribed me antianxiety medication at about this time, which helped, but I was still pretty freaked out by the diagnosis.

Had my relationship really been so horrible that I now had a psychological diagnosis to show for it?

Apparently it had. This was an overwhelming concept for me.

When it came to Russell, though, the change in him since we had begun therapy was evident, and again I had hope. Russell and I were now talking about our feelings at home, sharing them with each other. I was doing what had always been impossible for me, sharing how I felt in the moment. We were able to respect each other, and if we needed a mediator, we called Dr. Sophy.

The conversations between Russell and me were not always pleasant. There were many tense moments that we would not have been able to navigate alone, considering our history. But now, with a set of professional eyes on us at all times, we were not alone.

I was not alone.

We were soon attending treatment biweekly and sharing our feelings about the past, present, and future. I was starting to believe in us as a couple again. My hope seemed reasonable. I was with the man I loved, and he was really trying.

By this time, the other Housewives and I had begun filming the second season of the show. And I had a couple of pretty tough weeks after my diagnosis. On camera. Does a breakdown in Vail ring a bell?

I was excited to reunite with my castmates and to be busy with the hectic schedule of filming and doing publicity. I had been doing so much therapy between seasons that I was getting sick of hearing about myself. I was ready for some girl time.

As soon as I began spending more time with the girls again, however, I found that my renewed faith in my relationship with Russell created an unforeseen problem. The last time I had seen Camille, I had been complaining about how Russell had dislocated my jaw and vowing that I was finally ready to leave him. She had listened patiently and become invested in giving me advice and helping me to save myself from my marriage.

Now Camille saw me behaving like a Stepford Wife again, acting like everything was just great with Russell. This about-face in my behavior confused her. She didn't know what was going on with me, and her frustrations were brewing. She wasn't the only one. The constant back-and-forth was taking its toll on everyone around me. Those who loved and supported me and allowed me to cry on their shoulder countless times were reaching their boiling point as well.

Ironically, it was at a tea party when things finally boiled over.

Suddenly Camille burst out, "He hits you!"

Silence.

Once the words were spoken, I could almost see them hovering in the air right in front of Camille's mouth. Panic-stricken, I frantically wished there was a way to make them disappear. My face felt hot and my chest was pounding so hard that no anxiety medication in the world could have slowed it down.

The secret was out. Oh, God! Now what?

My thoughts raced forward. Although there were only five of us in the room, I knew the minute this hit the air, millions would know the truth.

How the hell was I going to weather this?

One thing was for sure, though: no matter what came, I wasn't ready to jump ship. I was so addicted to Russell and the chaotic pattern we had established that there was no way for me to leave until I was truly ready.

And honestly, things at home truly had seemed to be getting better.

I found myself at a stalemate: friends on one side, Russell on the other.

I knew something bad was going to happen and that Russell was not going to be happy. That meant things were about to get very complicated, especially for me.

The only way my friends could understand how I could possibly still be with Russell was if I was mentally ill or if he really wasn't as bad as I had claimed. They were starting to doubt me and to give up on me. I'm pretty sure they all had concluded that I was never going to leave Russell.

They couldn't understand what I was feeling: that if I just kept giving Russell as much love as I could, under even the worst circumstances, and I kept forgiving him, he would change eventually. The distance between my friends and me, which was visible in season two of the show, reminded me of that hollow feeling of abandonment I had experienced throughout my childhood.

At the time I was distraught by what I felt as their judgment of me. But now I can understand how frustrating my situation must have been for the housewives and my other friends. And I understand how impossible it is for anyone who hasn't experienced abuse to comprehend how incredibly complicated the dynamic between the abuser and the abused really is.

I had made a pact with Russell that I would keep our marital issues within the confines of our therapy sessions, so I put on a happy face for the outside world. Whenever anyone asked about our marriage, I said we were working on things and then quickly changed the subject. This wasn't always easy to do, considering that my marriage had become a common topic of conversation among my friends, but I did my best to zip my big lips. No matter what I did or did not say, my friends didn't believe for one minute that things were better with Russell, especially not after just a couple months of working on our marriage. They didn't particularly want to be around him, given all they had heard about his behavior before now. They were fed up with hearing me confess to all of the awful things Russell said and did to me, and then having to listen to me excuse away the abuse when he and I later reconciled.

I couldn't see it at the time because I didn't have any perspective on my relationship with Russell, or how it was impacting my friendships, but it was almost as if I were pulling my friends into the same cycle of abuse and violence in which I was trapped. Even if I wasn't ready to end the cycle, they were. They had long ago lost respect for Russell, and now they were beginning to lose respect for me because I stayed with him.

The challenges of my relationship with Russell bled onto our friendships in other ways, too. I was unreliable. On dozens of occasions I canceled dinner plans with my girlfriends at the last minute because Russell got pissed off about something. Even though he was still on his medication, his anger would sometimes spike. I would agonize about cancelling, but in the end I knew that if I went to dinner, Russell would become even angrier, and I would come home to a serious situation. So I'd cancel. This behavior continued to aggravate my already strained friendships. Things were a mess, and I was feeling pressure to find a solution that made everyone happy, including me.

There were nights when Russell and I would be out with another couple or group of friends and he would get upset over something insignificant. We would have to leave the restaurant abruptly. I never had the opportunity to explain to our friends—not that I could have made his behavior seem rational if I tried. Instead I made morning-after phone calls in an attempt to explain. I was tired of it all. I needed some peace.

Lisa Vanderpump would say to me, "You know what you need to do. You just don't have the strength to do it."

She was right. But I still had hope that Russell would change.

After five years with Russell, my personality had changed. I had almost become a shadow of myself. Because I was less bubbly and talkative, people thought I was disinterested or didn't like them as much as I once did. I was withdrawn when I was with Russell and anxious when I was without him. It was a never-ending roller coaster, and even worse, a course that could change at any turn. It didn't help that many of my friends had a difficult time being pleasant to Russell by this point. He could sense their animosity, and it made him angry at them—and, of course, at me.

But in some ways, for a while at least, our marriage actually was better than it had ever been. Dr. Sophy had given Russell and me some tools for talking about our feelings, and for the first time we started to communicate in more ways than just his shouts and my tears. Dr. Sophy encouraged me to attempt to discuss our emotions in the moment as they arose. This wasn't easy for me because I was used to putting Russell first and repressing my own reactions to his behavior. But I was so committed to saving our marriage that I dared myself to try.

It helped that Russell had begun to open up during our couples' therapy, so I was starting to see that he did in fact have a sensitive side. For the first time in Russell's life, he talked about how his childhood had affected him. For the first time I saw the pain he had experienced and the vulnerabilities it had created within him. I realized that for years I had had no idea who my husband really was. I was aware that his child-hood had made him strong and violent, but I didn't know that it had scarred him, too, or expect him to admit to this.

What was happening in our biweekly therapy sessions began to have an impact on our day-to-day life. One morning, as I was rushing around getting Kennedy ready for school, I heard the familiar sound of the front door slamming as Russell left for the office without a word.

He didn't say "good-bye," I thought. *He didn't say "I love you."*

Even though things had been better between us for several months at this point, I went into my default anxiety mode, wondering if I had done something to make Russell angry, and if he would explode at me when he got home. But this time I remembered what Dr. Sophy had told me about revealing my feelings to Russell and made a vow to give it a try. That night, after Kennedy was in bed, I went into the office where, as usual, Russell was working at the computer. I sat down on the brown couch near the big, ornately carved desk, which rested against a window that overlooked our backyard and pool.

"Do you have time to talk?" I said. "Because I want to let you know how I'm feeling. And if not, when can we do it later?"

This was so out of character for me that I could hardly look Russell in the eye as I spoke. But I started to relax when he nodded at me in encouragement.

"When you leave the house in the morning without saying 'good-bye' to me, it really bothers me," I said. "And I worry that I've done something to make you angry. And then, for the whole rest of the day, I have this horrible chest-pounding anxiety. It makes it hard for me to be in the moment with Kennedy when I'm distracted by my concerns and my anxiety, and then I end up feeling guilty about not being a good mom. Just a simple 'good-bye' and a hug would make it so much better for us."

Instead of lashing out in response to this observation, as I would have expected in the past, Russell listened calmly while I spoke.

"Sometimes I feel like you're so occupied with Kennedy in the morning that you don't have time for me," he said. "And you don't say 'Good morning' and 'I love you' to me, and so I leave angry and feeling like I didn't get what I needed from you."

I was as stunned as I'd ever been at something Russell had said to me. It had never occurred to me that Russell was insecure. I was the insecure one in our marriage. I was the anxious one.

"I'm sorry," I said.

But this was different from all the moments when I had apologized in the wake of his unjustified accusations, just to keep the peace and to keep him from hurting me or leaving. This apology was sincere because I really did feel bad that I had hurt his feelings, and even more than that, I felt my heart go out to him because of all of the ways in which he was so much more vulnerable than I had ever suspected.

"You know, if we would have had therapy six years ago, we wouldn't be in this place," he said.

Of course, the truth was that Russell needed therapy years and years before this moment, and so had I. But I was glad that he had acknowledged that our couples' therapy was necessary and might even do some good. I hoped that it wouldn't be too little, too late, to save our marriage and that it might even continue to improve it.

At the same time that I was optimistic, being in therapy helped me to recognize for the first time just how much distance had grown between Russell and me. Dr. Sophy had encouraged us to be more affectionate with each other to create closeness. When we tried to hold hands during our therapy sessions, it felt so foreign that we often weren't able to do it. Russell would take my hand in his, but it was such an awkward feeling that we would both let go. It was sad for me to realize that we had gone for so long without that kind of closeness that it now felt completely artificial. It was almost like our hands didn't fit together anymore.

Russell could definitely see the positive impact that the medication was having on his life and our marriage. He told Dr. Sophy that if he had had the medication ten years before, he wouldn't have caused so many problems for himself over the years, and that if he had taken the medication six years before, he and I never would have had the kinds of serious issues that had plagued our marriage.

But Russell was not happy, overall, with the medication's effect on him. He told me that it made him feel numb, and he worried that it took off his edge. This was potentially a major problem because he felt like his aggressive personality was necessary in his business. The medication made him feel more docile, and less able to tap into his inner pit bull. He felt like this put him at a disadvantage at a time when he needed his edge more than ever, because of how his business had suffered with the economy and the negative press that had come out about him during the first season of the show.

Russell never admitted it to me outright, but I also think that he began to feel like he was potentially dealing with more severe mental illness than he wanted to admit.

Of course, to complicate matters, we were living all of this out in front of the cameras during season two of the show. I still faced the cameras every day, no matter what was going on behind closed doors at home. In some ways, in spite of these pressures, I was happier with season two than season one because I felt like I became more relaxed in front of the cameras. I think I also was more comfortable with myself in general, probably as a result of my therapy. And it was possible during season two to see a lot more of who I really am as a person.

Now that we had Dr. Sophy in our lives, I at least had a framework for talking to Russell about his outbursts and letting him know that they weren't acceptable. In addition to our regular sessions, we began having conference calls with Dr. Sophy whenever we had an issue.

Not only was Dr. Sophy having a major impact on Russell, he also was finally helping me to find my voice. As I already mentioned, he started out by having me speak up for myself and express my feelings in small ways. From there, as I gained confidence, he actually got me to value myself enough that my abandonment issues no longer ruled me as completely as they had in the past. During a fight that spring, Russell went right to the default threat that he knew would scare me the most.

"That's it, I'm done," he said. "I'm out of here."

Instead of begging him to stay, as I once would have done, I thought about how Dr. Sophy had told me not to let Russell try to make it my fault that he was leaving. Rather, I was supposed to make him take responsibility for his own words and actions.

"If you want to leave, that's your decision," I said, as Dr. Sophy had coached me. "I'm not going to stop you. I don't want you to leave, but if you need to leave for you, then you should go ahead."

I wouldn't exactly say that Russell became all soft and cuddly after that, but my logical reaction to his threat definitely deflated its power and shifted the balance between us to a more equal place. As a lifelong conflict avoider who had let many friendships and relationships end rather than directly confront someone about even the smallest issue, or even decline an invitation to a party or movie, I was stunned by the fact that it was possible to speak up for myself. At thirty-nine years old, I was finally finding my voice.

Sometimes the process of becoming more confident and independent was still so uncomfortable for me that it was almost comical. One day when we were filming for season two, I was out to lunch with one of my girlfriends, Julie Waldorf. Because I was miked, filming and talking to Julie, I hadn't really been able to focus long enough to eat my salmon. The restaurant was busy with its lunch rush, and the waiter hurried over and cleared my friend's plate. He reached for mine.

"Are you finished?" he asked me.

"Okay, yes," I said, even though I had barely begun to eat.

The waiter took my plate and walked away.

"You can't even tell a waiter that you're not finished with your lunch," Julie said to me. "You need to figure out how to start speaking up for yourself."

I was surprised by her observation, but because Dr. Sophy had been talking about these issues so much, I knew she was right. Julie had been through enough tears with me to know what she was talking about. And because the moment was a clear indication of just how deep my fear of conflict went, I could see how much work I had to do. Rather than worrying that maybe the waiter was trying to finish his shift and needed me to pay so he could get his tip, I had to stop putting every-one else first and actually speak up for myself and my needs.

In that moment I came to realize that even baby steps would get me somewhere if I took enough of them.

When I found my voice, it did not go unnoticed by Russell. Again, we were in the office. He was sitting at the computer and had turned to look at me where I was sitting on the couch. We were talking about how he had yelled at me the night before.

"You're not going to treat me like this anymore," I said. "I can't live like this anymore."

"Like what?" he said, his voice spiking with anger.

I described what I hadn't liked about his behavior, almost critiquing him and the way he had acted, which was something that I had never done before. Now he was *really* mad at me.

"It's your fault," he said, his voice rising. "If you didn't do things to make me so mad, these kinds of things wouldn't happen."

"Let's get Dr. Sophy on the phone," I said. "Let's talk about this with him. Because I'm tired of you telling me that I bring this out in you and that it's all my fault."

Russell angrily threw down one of his favorite statements about our relationship.

"I'm driving this bus," he said. "If you think this is a relationship of equality, you're wrong. If you think this is fifty-fifty, you're wrong."

"I need fifty-fifty," I said. "I need this to be that kind of relationship because I can't live like this anymore. My anxiety is out of control, and I can't gain weight, and I'm just a mess all the time."

He looked at me in disbelief. Instead of becoming the weak

little lamb he had accused me of being, I was actually standing up for myself and expressing my needs like an adult woman.

"I have a voice now," I said.

"Yeah, you found your voice, and I'm not sure I like it," he said with a little smirk.

I started to laugh, and he did, too. Instantly the anger evaporated.

In that moment, the process by which we were both trying to heal our marriage and ourselves—as uncomfortable as it was—actually brought us closer together. But overall, I think Russell was deeply threatened by the shift in our relationship, even if it most often revealed itself in small changes like me saying I didn't feel like Indian food for dinner, when I had always let him choose what we ate. As Russell felt himself starting to lose control over me, I don't think he knew how to be with me anymore, and his rage began to escalate. And because I now called him out on his inappropriate anger, he just grew more furious. In these moments, the medication only did so much.

chapter ten

Please, Not in Front of Our Daughter

Twice that spring, Russell crossed a line that I had always vowed would be a deal breaker for me. The first time it happened, I had stayed home while Russell went out for dinner and drinks with some of his business associates, and I had let Kennedy fall asleep in the master bedroom with me. Later that night, Kennedy and I were both awoken when Russell stormed in and started screaming.

"Fuck you!" he screamed at me. "Get the fuck out of my life!"

Kennedy looked up at me, sleepy and confused, but clearly frightened. I put my arms around her and pulled her close to me, immediately wanting nothing more than to protect my little girl. Then Russell turned his attention to his daughter.

"Your mom's a whore!" he yelled. "Your mom's a bitch!"

Kennedy started to cry hysterically, now clearly terrified. My heart was racing, and I started to cry, too. But I was mad. This was the kind of thing that could really damage Kennedy.

It was one thing for Russell to take his anger out on me, but I loved our little girl more than anything else in the world, and this was unacceptable.

"Please don't do this in front of her," I said. "Please stop."

He whipped around on me and got right in my face.

"It's your fault!" he yelled.

Then he turned back to Kennedy.

"It's your mom's fault," he said. "You need to know that your mom's a whore. Your mom's a bitch."

Kennedy started screaming and crying harder. She was really bawling by this point. I wrapped my arms around her and tried to calm her and cover her head so she wouldn't have to see Russell or be exposed to his anger.

"Please, Russell, just stop," I said. "Please don't do this in front of her."

But he wouldn't stop. Just as it had always been before therapy, there was no reasoning with him now. His anger had consumed the rest of his personality completely.

"Fuck you!" he screamed.

Finally I had had enough. Without another word to Russell, I picked Kennedy up and took her into her room, my heart breaking for her because of what she had just witnessed, desperate to get her away to the only place that felt safe in our house. Kennedy and I were both crying as I shut the door behind us.

"Daddy's mean," she said. "Daddy's mean."

"I'm sorry," I said. "Daddy's upset."

That was a difficult moment for me because I didn't want her to dislike her dad, but I also didn't want her to believe that his behavior was in any way acceptable. It was a hard balance to find. We both climbed into Kennedy's bed and I held her close to me, trying to make up for what she had just experienced with all of the love I could give her. Finally I was able to calm her and get her to sleep. I don't think I ever really slept that night; I kept one eye on the door. Russell didn't come in.

I was devastated that the closeness Russell and I had achieved through therapy, and the calm that had seemed possible since he had gone on medication, had been shattered so suddenly. But now that he had been abusive in front of Kennedy, I had to face up to how his behavior could potentially affect her in the long term—I certainly didn't want her to repeat the patterns I had inherited from my mother—and I knew that I had to find a way to leave as soon as I could. Of course, it wasn't that easy. And, as always, I was one of my own biggest obstacles.

After that, Kennedy was even more determined to chaperone my interactions with Russell, never letting us be alone together. And she said something to me on several occasions when we were getting her ready for school in the morning that made me feel awful.

"Mommy, are you going to cry again today?" she asked.

I remembered how much I had hated to see my own mother cry when I was little, and how much her sadness had colored my childhood, and now I did my best to act cheerful until I could find a better solution.

I was definitely growing stronger, thanks to the support of Dr. Sophy. I also felt increasingly confident, thanks to the experience of being a part of a popular television show about a group of strong, successful women. But everything that was happening that year was creating a feeling of tremendous pressure on me. I had always felt able to control the abuse in my life, at least somewhat, as long as I had told only a handful of my closest friends. But now I had told more and more people. And I now grasped how severe Russell's mental illness probably was.

I was in the public eye, and I knew that if word of the abuse got out, it would spread like wildfire. I felt a tremendous amount of stress about the fact that I needed to do whatever it took to make sure this didn't happen. It was a full-time job for me to try to keep Russell under control, try to stay present with Kennedy and be a mom to her, and then try to come up with ways to manipulate our TV show to the extent I could. I also think that the constant anxiety of being recorded, watched, and criticized, and always trying to stay one step ahead of Russell's anger and attacks, was starting to take its toll on me after six years. This was when I really couldn't gain weight, no matter that I was eating and how much I was trying to maintain my health. My nerve endings were so raw that I often said I felt like the frayed end of a rope. And I couldn't stop thinking about the diagnosis of PTSD that I had been given by Dr. Sophy. Now that I was conscious of my condition and its symptoms, it was almost more than I could handle. I worried that there must be something really wrong with me, that I might be crazy. I was also deeply disturbed because the diagnosis gave me some real perspective on the severity of Russell's abuse and the damage it had done to me.

Worried about how to keep the abuse from being captured by the cameras—especially with the cameras on me constantly, and Russell in danger of exploding constantly—I was losing traction. It was like I was trying to hold the lid on a pot of boiling water. I struggled and struggled to keep everything contained, and then I lost control. When it happened, I essentially had a complete and total nervous breakdown, and the cameras were there to capture it, as shown in episode three of season two.

This six of us girls had gone to Vail for a ski trip, and we were staying at Camille's house there. After a long day of skiing, Kyle and I decided to have a glass of wine in the hot tub. Kyle and I are very close, and we ended up having an intense, heart-to-heart conversation. All of the emotional stress I had been dealing with started to bubble up.

As I said, I was so anxious throughout 2011 that I could barely eat, so I was really skinny. The combination of the emotions, and the wine, and the hot tub, and the altitude, on a day when I hadn't eaten and had spent hours skiing was all too much for me. When I got out of the hot tub, I didn't really know where I was anymore. I was upset and disoriented, and I couldn't find my makeup bag or my things. I started to feel scared, and it all became too much for me; I emotionally collapsed.

I began to try to hide from the cameras. It wasn't logical, but I didn't want anyone to see me. I tried to climb into a suitcase and cover myself up with the clothes inside. I was shaky and disoriented, and I wasn't aware of what I was saying, but I knew that something was wrong with me. While I wasn't entirely lucid, I remember bits and pieces of the night very clearly.

"You're having a nervous breakdown," Adrienne said.

That snapped me back to reality, but it didn't ease my anxiety. I was exhausted and run down, but long after we all went to bed that night, I couldn't sleep or stop myself from worrying. I was terrified of Russell and the signs that his physical violence was escalating, but I was so anxious about everything that felt out of control in my life that all I wanted was to be at home, even though that's where the problems were. I felt like I just needed to be in my own house, my own bed.

It didn't help that I was staying in Camille's daughter's room. There was a crib against one wall from when she had been a baby. It made me think of my own daughter, who I was so worried about just then, and it made me miss her and want to be with her. At the same time, I thought about Camille's daughter and son and how Kelsey and Camille's divorce must have impacted them. It was becoming increasingly clear to me that I was not going to be able to hold everything together and stay in my marriage. I felt incredibly guilty at the thought that my own little girl was going to lose her father through a divorce, and I worried about how all of this was going to impact her. I honestly don't know if I wanted to be with her for her, or for me, but even though it was the middle of the night, I wanted to go home.

That was obviously a really difficult experience for me. I didn't watch the episode about that night until after it first aired, and it was hard for me to sit through.

After we got back from Vail, I tried to keep up appearances for Russell, and for the show, but I remember that entire spring as being very tense. It felt like, at any moment, I was going to lose control of everything, and I was incredibly anxious about what would come next. It didn't help that Russell's business life seemed increasingly tenuous, but he would never be up-front with me about what our financial situation really was. From the beginning, he had purposely kept his business a complete mystery to me, and I had never asked for any details because I didn't want him to think I was a gold digger. All I knew about his business was how it affected his mood and what it led him to say about what we should or shouldn't buy.

One week, he'd say:

"Oh, my gosh, we're rocking at work. Things are going awesome."

Then he would say, "Oh, some deal didn't go through."

He'd be in a bad mood about it for two days, and then it would be, "I got this new client today. This is going to be the big one. This is going to be awesome."

Or, out of nowhere, he'd say, "We should get the new Bentley."

Later that week, we'd go look at Bentleys together, and I'd figure business must be good. Then the next week he would say it was a bad week, and I'd never hear another word about the Bentley again.

Next it would be, "I think we should buy a ski place in Deer Valley."

Finally, during the second season when all I knew for sure was that there was a tremendous amount of negative press about Russell, and that he had told me it was hurting his business, I got fed up.

"Do not promote me," I said. "Because it's confusing me. Stop saying we should do things if we can't. Because I don't know what's going on. I love you, and I don't care if we don't have a pot to piss in. Just tell me so we can go to a one-bedroom apartment."

I didn't realize it was anything more serious than Russell's tendency to be a natural salesman. And, of course, I had no idea what was really going on with our finances. In the back of my mind I still always figured that we had the $14 million trust to fall back on, the one he had promised me was in place for our family throughout our marriage. Now that I know the truth, it makes me so sad that Russell didn't feel like he could be honest with me, because I would have lived with him in our car if it had come down to it.

There were, however, some genuinely happy moments for my family that spring, which I hope people will remember, in spite of everything that's happened since. In May I threw a fifth-birthday party for Kennedy, several months after her actual birthday, when the weather was warm enough to celebrate outside. I know this event generated a great deal of controversy because of its $60,000 price tag. But the truth is that Russell and I certainly did not pay that much for the party. Some companies donated products for the event because it was filmed for the show. It was a really wonderful day for our family, and I was so happy to be there with my husband and all our friends celebrating our beautiful daughter's life.

Russell and I were also continuing to work on our marriage that spring. Our couples' therapy seemed to be going well, and I had hope. We had some major hurdles to overcome, though. The years of disrespect and abuse had taken their toll. I couldn't let my guard down with Russell, especially in the bedroom. Russell complained constantly that we were not having enough sex. Finally I went lingerie shopping, in hopes that a sexy costume would allow me to play a new role in the bedroom, let go of all the resentment I felt toward Russell, and rediscover the passion we had once had.

Having told me about smoking the most potent marijuana in the United States during his college years in Hawaii, Russell said that the drug had calmed his temper. This made me think. I hadn't grown up with pot, as other drugs were more prevalent in my high school. And I had always heard that pot makes people hungry and tired, which didn't sound like much fun to me. But to make Russell calm, I would have tried pretty much anything. So bring on the Mary Jane.

Russell and I smoked pot together for the first time that spring. Kennedy was with my parents for the weekend, so Russell brought some home for us to try. We sat out by the pool and gave it a shot. I coughed my lungs out. Then something happened. Once we were stoned, Russell became the man I had fallen in love with: sweet, affectionate, and loving. It was even better than I had hoped it would be.

We smoked together a handful of times, and every time, Russell once again became the charming man I had been crazy about early in our relationship. And the sex was amazing. When we were high, he wasn't scary. We were back in love again, making love, and it was passionate. Russell commented many times that pot was saving our marriage. For Mother's Day, Russell brought home a Tupperware container filled with marijuana buds. He knew that his calm demeanor while stoned was the greatest gift he could give me. He was trying anything he could to calm his demons. I appreciated the effort and enjoyed the chance to feel close to him in a way that I hadn't for so long. The only problem was that pot made me terribly paranoid. And obviously we couldn't be stoned all of the time. It was going to take more than that to keep us together.

So, in a second effort to rev up our sex life and save our marriage, I decided to go for hormone replacement therapy. Russell had told me many times that it wasn't normal that I didn't have a sex drive. Of course, things were different for him. He saw sex and emotions as two completely different animals. I didn't. My emotions were in turmoil when I was around him, and my body couldn't be fooled. But at the time, I wasn't able to see our relationship so clearly, and so I did anything I could think of to improve things.

I made an appointment with Dr. Uzzi Reiss, the best-known hormone specialist in Beverly Hills. He's a dream; a kind, loving, compassionate man who has helped so many women master the art of sexuality.

My first visit to his office was eye-opening. I filled out paperwork about my body's *every* function, from my dry eyes to the length of my menstrual cycle. This man now knew everything about me. For weeks following our first meeting, I collected all sorts of samples. I had blood drawn twice, peed in jugs, and swabbed my cheeks. I wasn't sure how to take all of this. All I had wanted was to be horny for my husband. Now I was a science experiment. But I was committed to making it work.

Then, once the samples were complete, we waited.

After the analyses came back from the lab, next came the lotions and potions; lotions of love, or so I hoped. Dr. Reiss explained that I was to use one cream on the back of my thigh twice a day. Then I was to take a handful of supplements throughout the day to balance my hormones. In one month I would be the vixen I used to be.

Great, I thought. *I will do whatever it takes to feel passion again.*

A few weeks in, I went to a trunk show at Neiman Marcus with a group of my gal pals. I was telling my friend Sharon about my new hormone regime when she looked at me cross-wise.

"It's not your hormones," she said. "It's that you don't like him. When are you going to get it?"

I heard her, but I didn't. I was still hoping that Russell and I could turn things around.

That June 10 was my fortieth birthday. Russell and I had planned a big night out with friends to celebrate, but that entire week was busy. The night before my birthday, Russell and I attended a fashion show at Adrienne Maloof's house to launch her new shoe line, which had turned out so amazingly. Of course, we were filming the event, which was very crowded. The producers had reserved seats for the housewives up front, while our husbands kind of had to fend for themselves. I was busy handling my role in the show, and Russell felt as though

I didn't pay enough attention to him. As soon as we left the event, he started in on me.

"You humiliated me," he said. "You didn't sit by me. You were trying to embarrass me."

"There were no seats," I said.

He had not calmed down by the time we got home. When midnight arrived—and with it, my fortieth birthday—he sneered at me.

"Happy birthday, asshole," he said. "Fuck you, you psychotic bitch."

My heart started to race. Russell had that familiar blank expression in his eyes, and I was fearful that his anger might escalate into violence. I texted Russell's exact words to Dr. Sophy because I felt like I needed him to know that something scary was starting to happen at our house. I told Russell that I had texted Dr. Sophy, so he knew that someone was monitoring the situation and his behavior, and asked Russell to sleep in another room. I went to bed in Kennedy's bedroom. I didn't sleep at all, though, because I kept expecting Russell to come in after me. He didn't, I think, because of the text I had sent to Dr. Sophy.

The next day, which was my birthday, Lisa and I flew to Las Vegas to tape us attending the bachelorette party for Lisa's daughter, Pandora. Russell called me, but I didn't take his call. I was tired of being insulted, and I knew that he wasn't calling with an apology. But I did text him later in the day, saying, "I love you. We're fine. I'm just working."

Even though I was feeling like we were far from fine at that point, I was doing whatever it took to keep Russell placated.

I just kept thinking about his words and the fact that, for the rest of my life, his insults would always be my first memory of my fortieth birthday. And these harsh words had come from the man I loved. It would have been heartbreaking to me once, but I was growing numb to the offensive things he said after so many years of verbal abuse. His barbs weren't penetrating my heart like they once had. Now they just made me feel sad for us.

Part of the bachelorette celebration, all of which was filmed, took place in one of the casinos featuring the Chippendales dancers. Now, they could not be further from the type of guy I like—brainy businessmen with glasses—but of course this was Las Vegas. Russell had actually teased me earlier in the week about my new oiled-up, shirtless boyfriends. It had been clear that he knew, as well as I did, that there was no real threat there. Lisa and I were only attending that night as the chaperones for her daughter's bachelorette party, and although we know how to have a good time, this was not exactly our cup of tea. While I didn't leave with a chipmunk—as Lisa called them—the Chippendales show was lots of fun, and Lisa and I did have some laughs.

After the show, all of us girls went to dinner, cameras in tow. They had a dessert sent to the table for my birthday, which I appreciated, considering the birthday gesture I had received from Russell. When dinner was over, we hit the casino's club for a little bit of typical bachelorette party dancing—with cameras, of course.

Finally, it was getting late, and Lisa and I were exhausted. We left the young bachelorettes to their fun and went back to our rooms to sleep. When I settled into my room, I realized I no longer had my cell phone. I phoned our casino host and requested that he check the restaurant and club security and notify me if he found it. I then called my assistant, Julie, to let her know I didn't have a phone, and to call me on the hotel line if she needed me or if anything urgent happened. Then I happily put myself—and my tired, high-heel-wearing feet—to bed.

I awoke at 4:00 a.m. to the loud ringing of the hotel phone and an angry voice on the other end.

"Where have you been?" Russell bellowed.

"What?" I answered groggily.

"I have been calling you all night!"

Oh, no, here we go.

"You have been out all night fucking the Chippendales!" he screamed.

"What are you talking about?" I said, finally standing my ground a little bit. "I was sound asleep. I was with Lisa all night, and we were filming. You have got to be kidding me. We are not doing this. This is ridiculous."

I finally managed to calm Russell down, but it felt like an uneasy peace. The girls and I flew back to Los Angeles the next day and we belatedly celebrated my birthday with a large group of friends that night. I was a little bit nervous about seeing Russell because things had been so tense between us for the past two days, but he ended up surprising me. And this was yet another instance when we had one of the best nights of our marriage, followed by one of its worst, most violent moments.

Russell had gotten a beautiful one-bedroom suite for us at

the Four Seasons, and Kennedy was at home with Gloria, so it was just the two of us. While we were getting ready for dinner, Russell pulled me down on the couch next to him and handed me a card. I smiled at him and opened the envelope. When I started to read the outside, I was floored:

"Believe it or not, I know that I'm not always the easiest person in the world to get along with. There are times when I'm moody, and no matter what you do or say, I'll find fault. . . . Well, it's not you. It's me. I just can't understand what someone as wonderful as you could see in me, and I get scared. I'm afraid you'll suddenly see all my flaws and fall out of love with me."

I opened the card and read the rest of its preprinted message:

"I know it's no excuse, but those times when I'm the most difficult are probably the times I'm loving you the most and can't bear the thought of life without you."

And then I read the words that Russell had written inside:

"This is the first time in my life that I was able to find a card that expresses <u>exactly</u> how I feel. I love you so much that I live in constant fear that I'm going to one day lose you. In truth, it's a bittersweet feeling to love one as much as I love you. Yes I live in fear but the love I feel for you is wonderful and something I had never experienced until I met you. . . . Stay positive and never give up. We have so much to look forward to." He had signed his message from himself and all the kids, and added this at the end: "And God Bless Dr. Sophy!!!"

It was everything I had ever wanted to hear.

We're going to turn this around, I thought.

Russell had never apologized to me like this before. The closest he had ever come to admitting that he could be a bad guy almost had a note of braggadocio to it. "I'm an asshole," he would say. "Let's be honest. You're probably married to the most difficult human being on the planet."

Sometimes he even used this as a kind of pep talk when I was nervous about something in my life.

"I'm an asshole," he would say. "If you can deal with me, then you can deal with anybody."

But for the first time ever, here he was, taking ownership for how he had treated me over the years, and apologizing, and really wanting to put the past behind us, start anew, and be a better partner to me.

I was happier than I'd been since Russell and I had first dated. Even when my daughter was born, which will always be the greatest blessing of my life, the joyous event was overshadowed by the physical abuse that had begun while I was pregnant. But now I had real cause to hope.

We took about twenty friends out to dinner, and we were all eating and drinking and having the best time. After dinner, we went to Beecher's Madhouse, which is like an adult freak show, and so much fun. All twenty of us were there, and we had front-row seats; everyone was drinking and laughing and having the most amazing time. I really felt like Russell was making an effort to show me that he cared, and to celebrate with me and all of our friends. He was letting me be myself, and it felt really good to be there with him. I looked around at one point and felt so grateful that the bad times were finally over.

We have all of these friends, I thought. *It's sad that we've been through so much heartache, but maybe everything is going to change for us.*

At the end of the night, Russell and I were dancing and kissing, and I was actually feeling some of the long-lost butter-flies I'd once had for him swarming inside me again. The entire night was perfect—that is, until Russell and I were alone.

When we got back to our hotel, we went into the bedroom of our suite and left my assistant, Julie, sleeping out in the liv-ing room area. Russell and I were both in a good mood from the fun night we had just enjoyed. We got into bed and started kissing. Then he pulled back and looked at me.

He started asking me detailed questions about what had happened when I was filming in Las Vegas the previous night. Like so many other times in our relationship, Russell had fabricated a story in his mind about how I had been with another man.

"You have bruises all over your back from fucking the Chip-pendales," he said.

"I don't have any bruises," I said. "I know I don't."

"You're just a whore," he said.

"I wasn't with anyone last night," I said. "I was with women—filming—all night. Then I went home. There were cameras with me the whole time. You can look at what I did."

We were both naked in bed, he was lying on his back, and I was leaning over him, trying to reason with him, even though I should have known better than to even try to talk to him when he was mad. He raised up on one elbow and punched me, hard, in the right eye.

The pain was excruciating.

I hit him back. I didn't care that he had told me never to do that again because he might kill me if I did. I was hurt. And fed up.

I put my hand over the right side of my face. Then I uncovered it and opened my eye. I could tell that something was very wrong with my vision. This whole time, Russell was glaring at me.

"You're so dramatic," he said. "You're fine."

I tried to shake off the pain and lie back down. But I could tell that something was *really* wrong. I got up and went out into the living room area and woke up Julie.

"He hit me," I said.

"Are you okay?" she asked, looking at my eye.

Before I could say too much, Russell came out and started calming me down and convinced me to go back to bed.

I was in so much pain.

"You really hurt me this time," I said. "You really hurt me."

"You're fine," he said. "You're just being a drama queen."

Of course, there was no calling an ambulance. And with pain that extreme, there was no sleeping. I was devastated. Even though I had been working up the strength to leave Russell for months, and I should have known better than to get pulled in again by this point in our marriage, his card had given me hope that maybe he had changed, and maybe we could still work things out.

I had let my guard down again, only to get disappointed *again*. Although I was accustomed to the emotional cycle of the abuse—how the little glimpses of good made me willing to take some of the bad in hopes that we'd have even more good—it didn't make it hurt any less when the bad came. And I was running low on hope by that point.

The next morning, I had a stabbing pain in my eye, and I couldn't look down or inward. But I tried to pretend that everything was fine, and went out by the pool to relax. As we were lying in the chaise longues, it became increasingly clear that everything was *not* fine. I still couldn't look down. I turned to Russell nervously. I knew he wasn't going to respond well, but I couldn't ignore how serious my injury was.

"Russell, I can't even move my eye," I said.

"You're just overexaggerating," he said.

By the end of the day, my eye still hadn't bruised, and so I started to think that maybe I *was* exaggerating the extent of my injury. As usual, Russell was so masterful at convincing me of whatever he wanted me to believe that it was almost like his thoughts had become my thoughts. But no matter what Russell said, he couldn't change the fact that my vision was impaired and I still couldn't look down.

I had just had LASIK surgery, so my vision should have been perfect in both eyes. The next day, I went to the doctor who had done my LASIK surgery. Russell went with me to my appointment, and on the way there, he told me what I should say to the doctor.

When we got to my doctor's office, Russell came into the examining room with me, giving me a warning look.

"I'm in a lot of pain, and my vision is blurred," I said.

The doctor examined my eye. The flap that had been raised up to fix my lens during my LASIK surgery was wrinkled, so he told me I would need to get a flap repair. We scheduled it for later that week.

"How did this happen?" my doctor asked.

I looked over at Russell, and my assistant, Julie, who also was in the room. Then I looked down, wincing at the pain.

"My daughter kicked me in the eye," I said.

"Really?" my doctor said. "What kind of shoes does she wear?"

I looked at Julie. Of course, she knew exactly what had happened and that I hadn't even seen Kennedy that weekend because she had been home with her nanny. But Russell was watching both of us very closely. It was an incredibly uncomfortable situation.

"Oh, you know, just normal kids' shoes," I said.

"She was on a swing," I added, trying to make the story more convincing.

"Really?" he pressed me. "So, she hit you with her back? Or why were you in front of her swing?"

"Well, I mean, I was just walking by the swing," I said.

"You should get your kid some new shoes," he said.

I felt terrible blaming the injury on something Kennedy had done, even accidentally. But I didn't want Russell to go to jail, and I knew that he would have if I told the doctor the truth. Plus, the extent of my injury had made me more scared of Russell than ever before.

The wrinkled flap explained my impaired vision, but I was

in so much pain that I wasn't convinced that was the extent of my injuries.

"I'm in a lot of pain, and I'm having trouble looking down," I said.

My doctor gave me some pain medication and suggested I consult an ocular plastic surgeon. Every time I went back for my follow-up appointments at the LASIK center, Russell left his office to show up in time to make sure I was never alone with my doctor.

The day of my flap repair surgery, Russell again accompanied me. After surgery, the doctor put me in a darkened recovery room and told me not to open my eye for an hour.

"I'm fine," I said to Russell. "You can go."

Julie was in the waiting room, and I would have preferred to have her drive me home. Russell nodded and left the room. I closed both eyes and dozed off a little. When I opened my uninjured eye about ten minutes later, Russell was sitting in the room, staring at me.

I jumped.

"What did you tell him?" Russell asked.

"I told him what you told me to tell him," I said.

He stayed for the rest of the time I was there, just to make sure I didn't tell anyone how my eye had really been injured.

Russell even had the nerve to try to lie to Dr. Sophy about how I had been hurt.

"She ran into my hand," Russell said.

Of course, I had already told Dr. Sophy the entire story, and he knew better than to believe Russell. But when Dr. Sophy told me about Russell's explanation for the incident, I felt queasy. That was the same lie Russell had told me early in our relationship to explain away his arrest for domestic violence against his first wife. Even when he was cornered, Russell still thought he could lie his way out of any problem.

chapter eleven

"It's Over"

After my flap repair surgery was completed, I could see again, but I still couldn't look down. I had found an ocular plastic surgeon whose partner happened to be a craniofacial reconstructive surgeon. But first I had to wait ten days for my flap repair to heal. During this time, the doctors could not further examine my eye, and so they didn't yet know the severity of my injury. The mood at home between Russell and me was uneasy at best. We talked once again about how he had *really* hurt me *this* time, and the undeniable fact that our marriage wasn't working.

And then, on June 26, I was finally able to get a CAT scan to assess the full damage he had done to my eye. It revealed that 40 percent of my orbital floor, the bone that supports the eye, had been fractured. Not only that, but my muscle was trapped in the fracture, and that's why I was having so much pain when I looked down.

"You need to have orbital reconstructive surgery," my doctor said. "I'm going to tag-team it with a craniofacial plastic surgeon. This is major surgery. You'll need to spend the night at Cedars-Sinai. This is not a small thing."

I studied the MRI. There was the proof of all that I had suffered at Russell's hands. I thought back to the Super Bowl and how hard he had hit me that night. I thought back to the two times he had screamed at me in front of Kennedy while I begged him to stop. I hadn't wanted to admit it, but things had been escalating for the past six months.

I can't believe that I've allowed myself to stay in a situation that has become this dangerous, I thought.

I realized that Russell could have killed me, or that having done that much damage inside my eye, he could have blinded me.

My doctor went on to tell me that I would need a titanium implant beneath my eye. In the best-case scenario, everything would be fine. But there was a chance that, even after the surgery, my eye would be sunken for the rest of my life. Hearing that I was in danger of having a lifelong deformity from something that Russell had done to me was enough to finally snap me out of the spell that Russell had over me. I guess, for me, having radiographic evidence of the amount of injury I had sustained was what it took for me to feel like I was justified in leaving. I knew, without a doubt, that I had to get away from Russell before something worse happened and it was too late.

When Julie and I got home from my doctor's appointment, I told her to pack her things, along with a bag for Kennedy. I was nervous as I moved around the bedroom of the Bel Air home I had shared with my husband for more than two years. I kept thinking that I heard Russell coming in the front door, although I knew he was at the office.

Even after everything Russell had put me through, I felt sad as I saw his suits in the closet while packing what I would need. But most of my memories in that room were unhappy— scenes of him screaming at me, belittling me, intimidating me. I had long ago given up on believing in the love he claimed to feel for me—every time he called me a whore or beat my head against the side of the car—but I still loved him, and I had never wanted to get a divorce.

I was heartbroken because of all I had been through and because I finally had to admit that I could not make Russell be the man I needed him to be. I had stuck it out for as long as I possibly could, hoping I could somehow fix him or fix our marriage, and I was devastated that I had not been able to do so. In addition, I was afraid of what it would be like to live without Russell and anxious about my financial situation. At the same time, I knew I couldn't stay any longer, and finally I was completely resolved to leave.

Even if life is hard by myself, it has to better than this, I thought.

And a part of me felt relieved that the panic, and dread, and pain might finally be over. Julie and I loaded our bags into my Escalade and picked up my daughter from camp. When I told Kennedy that we were going to stay at the St. Regis in Laguna Beach for the weekend, and that her grandmother would be joining us, she was thrilled. She loves spending the night at hotels, and, of course, being with her grandmother. Because my mother lives in Orange County, we used to do this weekend trip often, so nothing seemed out of the ordinary to Kennedy. I didn't mention her father and she didn't ask.

When we got to the hotel, Julie and my mom took Kennedy down to the pool, and I called Russell. I hadn't wanted to call him before we got to Laguna because I had been afraid he would try to follow me. But when I got him on the phone and told him about my eye and the extensive surgery it would require to repair it, he remained calm. I think he realized in that moment what I had just realized: He had pushed me past the point of no return.

"It's over," I said. "I need you to move out."

"I'll be out by tomorrow," he said.

And that was it.

I think Russell had been expecting this. He knew what he had done this time, and he knew he could go to jail for a year for what he had done to me. I was feeling so many emotions— sadness, anger, fear, relief—and I felt lucky to have so much support with me that weekend.

Next, I called my girlfriends. All of the Housewives were together in Hawaii on vacation. I had been upset that I wasn't able to go on the trip with them, because they had recently said that they didn't want to film with me if it meant risking Russell's wrath. I was unhappy to miss the holiday, which I knew would be fun, and that Russell had created yet more tension between us. I was angry at Russell because this was yet another example of his ongoing inability to control himself with friends and business associates; and therefore, yet another reminder of why I needed to leave him and get on with my life.

I wanted the girls to know that I was safe, but I don't think that's the only reason I called them. I was well aware that once I told them I was leaving Russell, there'd be no going back. I had already lost enough of their respect by this point, and I knew that if I decided to return to him again, especially after the severity of the injury I had sustained this time, they would not be willing to be a part of my life anymore.

"It's over," I said. "I asked him to move out."

The tone of their voices suggested that they doubted I'd really go through with it. They had heard me complain about things Russell had done and vow to leave him in the past, so they couldn't be sure that this time would be any different. But unlike me, they hadn't seen the MRI and didn't know about the titanium implant. I didn't want to go into too many details over the phone, so I just told them the basics. I was certain that I was really leaving Russell and could tell them the rest later.

Russell called and tried to talk to me several times that weekend, but I really was done. I've always wondered if he thought there was a chance that we could get back together, but I knew there wasn't. I told him that I didn't want to speak to him and needed time away.

We stayed in Laguna two extra days because I was nervous about going back home. I wasn't sure that Russell would really be gone. If he was, I was scared about how it would feel to stay in the house alone and to begin my life without him. As I turned my key in the lock of the Bel Air home we had shared and entered its silent rooms, I felt anxious, but I smiled and tried to act normal for my daughter. I was hoping, at least, that this change would be positive for her, and I wanted her to be excited about her new life.

Russell was gone.

When I went upstairs to our room, all of his clothes were gone. I walked into the bathroom; all of his toiletries were gone. It was like he had barely lived there with me.

The hardest thing for me to get used to was sleeping by myself at night. As I said, I've always had terrible nightmares and hated to sleep alone. Sometimes I honestly think that's part of the reason I always needed to be in a relationship. My mom came and stayed with me, and Julie was there, too, and Gloria, and of course the house had an alarm system, but I was still nervous in those weeks of our separation. After all Russell had put me through and what I knew he was capable of, it was difficult for me to feel safe. I had all of the locks changed and got new, computerized keys made that can't be reproduced. But many nights I lay awake in bed while my daughter slept beside me, afraid that Russell might go out drinking and get angry enough to come to the house. If he did, I knew he would be able to get in.

But Russell never threatened me during this time, as many abusers do when the abusive relationship finally ends. I think he knew that, ironically, his abuse had made me stronger, and that after what had happened with my eye, I wasn't going to tolerate any more threats or violence from him.

———————

I DON'T THINK I realized how much Russell had been affected by the last incidence of abuse or the fallout from it. About two weeks after he moved out, Russell brought his son Griffin over to see Kennedy. They were going to go out and do something together, but she didn't want to go with Russell, so we decided that we would all stay at the house, and the kids would swim in the pool. While the kids were outside with the nanny, Russell and I tentatively caught up on what had been going on in both of our lives.

"Oh, by the way, do you want to see the MRI?" I said.

"Yeah, sure," he said.

When he looked at the MRI, and he could see the fracture and the muscle herniating through the fracture, he started to weep. In all of the time I had known him, I had never seen him cry.

"I had no idea how badly I hurt you," he said. "I had no idea. I thought you were just exaggerating. I didn't know."

I stood there in disbelief.

"I love you more than I love my own children," he said. "I love you more than I love any person I've ever loved in my entire life. And I cannot believe I've done this to you."

He sat down somberly. I was too shocked to say anything.

"I don't know how we got here," he said. "I just don't know how things got this bad."

ON JULY 5, 2011, my mom drove me to Cedars-Sinai for my orbital reconstruction surgery. As I lay in the pre-op area, I felt sad that Russell wasn't there to support me, but I knew that he couldn't be, and I reminded myself that he was the person who had caused me to need this surgery in the first place. Of course, my mom was with me, but hospitals make her nervous, so that added to the general mood of anxiety in the room.

I was scared, and all of the release forms I had to sign didn't help. I would be undergoing general anesthesia, and I worried that if something happened to me during the procedure, Kennedy would be left in Russell's care without me there to watch over her. I also was concerned that something might happen during the surgery that would cause me to lose my eye or become blind or disfigured. But I really liked my doctor, and he was very calming about the whole thing, and I tried to relax as best as I could.

When I came out of surgery, I was on the eighth floor at Cedars-Sinai. Although I was on morphine and pretty much out of it, I soon had cause to feel even more anxious. New nurses were coming in throughout the day as the shifts changed, and I could see that they all recognized me.

How am I ever going to keep this out of the press? I thought.

I knew there was nothing I really could do, so I tried not to think about it. That evening, I rested in my bed with ice on my eye. Although I was still on pain medication, I was alert and aware of what was going on in the room around me. Dwight and my mom were keeping me company.

Right before visiting hours ended for the night, Russell walked into my room holding a vase of red roses. I wasn't expecting him to just show up like that, and I was scared as soon as I saw him. My first thought was that there was no lock on my hospital room, and that he might be there to kill me, so that what he had done to my eye wouldn't come out in the press. My mom and Dwight were both furious with Russell for what he had done to me, and the mood was very tense.

"Why are you here?" I asked him.

Russell set down the roses and turned to my mom.

"I just want to apologize for hurting Taylor like this," he said. "I just feel awful, and I'm really sorry. I never meant to hurt her. The show pushed me to do this to her."

My mom was looking at him coldly, and I could tell she didn't have any idea what to say to him. Finally, she spoke.

"There's no excuse for what you've done to her," she said.

"I know that you must hate me for this," he said. "I love her and I'm so sorry."

My mom didn't say anything more to him. But Dwight was angry.

"Why are you here?" Dwight asked.

Russell turned to me.

"I want to stay and be with you," he said.

It was a really hard moment for me because, again, there was a part of me that really wanted him to stay. He was in a suit as usual and I couldn't help but think that he looked handsome. Even in that moment, I wanted him back. But when I looked at my mom and Dwight and saw how upset they were on my behalf, even if I still had difficulty mustering such care for myself, I realized it was inappropriate for me to allow Russell to be there when I was recovering from what he had done to me. I slowly shook my head NO.

Russell was determined, though.

"I just want to stay here tonight," he kept saying.

"No, you can't," I said.

I could tell that he was genuinely remorseful, but I also had images flashing through my mind of him getting angry during the middle of the night and putting a pillow over my face while I was on morphine and unable to defend myself. Finally, visiting hours were over, and it was time for Russell to leave. He looked sad and nervous as he turned toward the door.

"I'll let you get some sleep," he said. "I just wanted to see you. I was worried about you."

Again, it was a struggle for me as I watched him go because I wanted to have someone be there for me when I was hurt, but I knew that it couldn't be him, even though I loved him.

———

THIS WAS A VERY stressful time for me and for Russell. We were both worried about what would happen when my injury came out in the media. Even though I was not planning to press charges, Russell was terrified that the district attorney might, and that he would end up going to jail. That fear weighed heavily on his mind, as it did on mine. I still didn't want him to go to jail, even though he had hurt me so much. We also were trying to figure out the details of our separation. We agreed to do our best to remain a family for the kids. That was very important to Russell, and he talked about it frequently.

"Let's still spend holidays together," he said.

"I want that, too," I said. "I don't want to live my life without you. But it's too dangerous for me to live it with you."

That was the truth. I had come to love Russell's sons, and I knew that they were an important part of Kennedy's life. I wanted to do my best to ensure that we were still able to do things as a family. At the same time, it was incredibly painful for me to see Russell. I still loved him deeply, and with my feelings of loss amplified by my lingering abandonment issues, I felt like my heart was being ripped out every time I had to face the fact that he was no longer mine.

The next time I saw Russell after my surgery, I brought Kennedy over to his house so she could spend some time with him. It was so hard for me when I walked in; there he was, looking as polished and confident as ever in an impeccable suit. Everything about him was the same, only our relationship had changed.

When it was time for me to leave, Kennedy didn't want to stay without me, so we decided that the three of us would have dinner at a Mexican restaurant near Russell's new house. Later that evening, Russell needed to go to the airport in Burbank, which wasn't far from the restaurant, and I offered to drop him off after dinner.

As the three of us sat down at our table in the restaurant, it felt so normal, and yet I was keenly aware that we were no longer the family we had once been. I began to cry softly throughout the whole meal. When our food came, I couldn't eat because I was so upset.

"It's okay, honey, don't cry," Russell said. "I hope that we can still be a family. You are my family, and I want it to stay that way. I want us to be best friends."

"I want that, too," I said.

I smiled at him and tried to stop my tears for Kennedy's sake.

"Mommy, are you crying?" she said.

"No, I have allergies," I said. "My eyes are just watering."

She knew better than that. She kept asking me if I was crying, and I kept telling her that it was just allergies. After dinner, we dropped Russell off at the airport, and she and I both hugged him. As I drove away, I was wondering how we were going to possibly make this work.

How am I going to continue to see him like this? I thought. *And how am I ever going to get over him?*

About once a week, I brought Kennedy to Russell's house and we went and played in the park as a family, or took her out to dinner. Every time we said good-bye, I was devastated all over again.

I can't believe I have to go through thirteen years of coparenting with him after all we've been through, I thought.

Sometimes after we saw each other, I couldn't resist texting him:

"This is so hard. I miss you so much."

He often texted those types of messages to me, too, but we both knew it was really over this time. And so I focused on trying to end my romantic love for him and focus on my familial and friendship love.

At the same time, I was taking the first tentative steps toward getting a divorce. I had a great deal of anxiety about this because of the many times Russell had threatened me about how financially and personally devastating he would ensure our divorce would be for me, should it happen. Although we were getting along well, those warnings echoed in my mind. Matters weren't helped any when I spoke to a divorce attorney friend who told me that if I had to hire a forensic accountant to determine Russell's worth, it could cost me $200,000, not to mention that the attorney's billable hours could equal $100,000.

I decided to try being up-front with Russell about all of this.

"We can both hire attorneys, which I'm not going to be able to afford, and then I'm going to have to ask you to pay my attorney fees," I said. "Or you can just agree to these basic bills that need to be paid around here, for let's say a year, and then we'll be done."

Russell was open to the idea, so I sat down with all of the household bills. This was a scary experience for me because Russell had always controlled our finances and I had never been allowed to look at any of the bills, let alone what kind of assets we had to pay them. It wasn't that the bills themselves were that excessive, but because Russell had filed for bankruptcy before our marriage, he had put all of the bills in my name—even the Mercedes he drove.

I suddenly realized that if Russell decided not to pay these bills, everything would fall on me, and *my* credit would be destroyed. Since he had threatened to bankrupt me so many times in the past, if we ever divorced, I felt like I had good reason to be afraid of what he might do, even though he was acting nice for now.

I never worried that Russell wouldn't be able to support Kennedy and me, even though I knew he was already responsible for two other children. He had often reminded me about the family $14 million trust, and that if anything happened to him, we would be taken care of forever. On top of that, I was used to seeing him drop $1,500 to $2,000 on dinners for big groups of business associates several times a week. Compared to that, I felt like the basics that I wanted him to cover would be nothing.

I took the numbers over to Russell's house and nervously showed them to him. He looked through the pages for a few minutes, then looked at up me and nodded.

"Okay, yeah, no problem," he said. "That's fine."

I was so relieved as I drove home that night. I had my freedom, and maybe everything else would work out well after all. And then, the next day, Russell called me.

"I think maybe we should get attorneys involved," he said.

My heart sank. I had seen him threaten other people with lawsuits often during our marriage. He loved to play that bully role, and I felt like he was doing this to me now because he knew I couldn't afford the attorney fees for as long as he could. I figured he would come back later and offer me half of the money I had asked for, just so I'd feel lucky to get even that. At first I was overwhelmed and scared. All of my fears were coming true, and I didn't know how I would support myself or my daughter. And then something new happened. I got mad. I was tired of being bullied. I had left him. And I wasn't going to let him do it anymore.

"Why did you tell me 'Yes' last night, so I could go home with peace of mind, and this morning, you call and tell me we should get attorneys involved?" I said.

"I'm not going to do what you brought over last night," he said.

I snapped.

"You know what?" I said. "I just want you out of my life. You don't have to give me a dime. But I want you to leave Kennedy and me alone. I don't want to have to deal with seeing you anymore. I don't want Kennedy to have to see you. If you'll just leave us alone, I won't ask you for alimony. I won't ask you for any child support."

Of course, Russell didn't want that because then he wouldn't have had any control over me.

―――――――

AT ABOUT THIS TIME I started to see a more vulnerable side of Russell that I hadn't even known was there. By the end of July, the press had gotten ahold of the story about my orbital fracture and how it had happened. Soon after that, the story of Russell's arrest for the domestic abuse charges against his first wife came out. And then a news story surfaced that really got my attention. Apparently, in filings connected with her application to change Russell's visitation arrangement with his son, Russell's first wife stated that someone had seen Russell slap their son, Aiden. I wasn't sure it was true because I had never seen Russell even come close to harming any of his children, including Aiden, but it still scared me that the children—and especially Kennedy—might have been closer to danger than I had ever known.

The media coverage was relentless in its negative portrayal of Russell. That would have been bad enough, but because Russell's business was so much about the confidence he could inspire in investors, he was losing clients and increasingly unable to attract new ones. I didn't take any pleasure in this. It was embarrassing for me to have people know how much I had put up with for so long. And even more than that, I still loved Russell, and I felt terrible for him, especially because I could tell that all of these pressures were having a negative impact on him.

I wanted to help Russell. I made some calls to friends and came up with three possible solutions for him. I told him that he didn't have to worry about Kennedy and me, that I would take care of our daughter forever, and that he should just focus on taking care of himself. I figured we still had the $14 million trust to fall back on, but I wasn't even really thinking about money at that point. I knew we'd survive somehow.

The first option was for him to go to an in-house anger management treatment program in San Francisco, which would be paid for on his behalf. When he came out, he could acknowledge that he had behaved badly and that he had needed help for his emotional issues. And once he got that treatment, he could become an advocate for men with anger management problems. I even offered to go on a PR tour with him, so we could tell our story and help people together. I thought this was the best option, because I was already thinking about how I might be able to create something positive out of all I had been through, going back to when I was a child, and public speaking and advocacy seemed like a promising direction for both of us.

The second and third options involved going away to Mexico or Costa Rica for six months. A friend of ours has a private resort in Mexico and offered to let Russell stay there for six months while he figured out his next move. Another friend had a beautiful home in Costa Rica that he wasn't using and made a similar offer.

Another suggestion I had was for him to just go to St. John, which was our favorite island in the world, and be a bartender for six months. I thought if he could simplify his life—live in a one-bedroom apartment, shake cocktails, watch the sun rise and set, surf, snorkel, reconnect with the natural world—the experience could be really good and healing for him. We'd figure everything else out when he got back.

But Russell wanted to stay and make a stand, and I respected that.

chapter twelve

The Worst Day of My Life

I was doing my best to start rebuilding my life, and I assumed that Russell was doing the same. Then, in mid-August, he sent me a text asking if we could have a meeting the following Monday. I wrote him back to agree and let him know that I would be in his office at 2:00 p.m. that day.

I had a 1:00 meeting scheduled that day followed by the meeting with Russell. When I went into the office for my first meeting, I glanced into Russell's office and saw that the door was shut and the lights were off. That struck me as odd because he never missed a day at the office, but then I figured he had probably gone out for a lunch meeting. When my meeting was over, an hour later, his door was still shut, and the lights were still off. I started to be concerned until I saw that the light was on in the conference room. I peeked in the doorway, expecting to see Russell. But instead I found a business friend of ours doing some work.

"Have you seen Russell?" I asked. "We had a meeting."

I was starting to feel anxious because Russell never would have missed a meeting with me, even if he were angry. And he had no reason to be mad, as we were generally getting along.

"No," she said. "I was trying to reach him over the weekend, but I never heard from him."

This seemed so unlike him that I began to worry that something was wrong. A heaviness descended on my chest, but I didn't want her to see my concern, so I just smiled and waved as I turned and walked down the hallway. I tried to reach Russell on his phone and sent him several text messages about the fact that he had missed our meeting. As anxious as I was, I kept my tone light and jokey, in case it was nothing.

"Forgot about me already," I wrote.

As I got into my car to leave, I kept calling him, but every time I did, it went straight to his voice mail. I knew that's what happened if Russell were on another call, so I tried to tell myself that this was the explanation. But I couldn't escape the feeling that something wasn't right. He wasn't clicking over to say he'd call me right back. He wasn't answering my texts. I thought of all the possible explanations: Maybe he had taken a last-minute trip and forgotten to tell me; maybe he had gotten caught in another meeting; maybe he had lost his phone; maybe he had met a woman over the weekend. I didn't like this last possibility at all, but at least it would be an explanation. Still, I couldn't shake my fear that something was terribly wrong, and my anxiety was starting to build.

I called several of our mutual friends, with whom Russell was usually in touch, to see if they had heard from him. None of them had. I called Dr. Sophy and asked him to check in with Russell, because I knew he had been texting and calling Russell and me every day during our separation. Dr. Sophy told me that he hadn't heard from Russell, either. I still thought it was possible that Russell was just mad at me for something I didn't know I'd done—it obviously wouldn't have been the first time—so I asked Dr. Sophy to check in, just to get a response, so we'd both know Russell was okay.

It was almost time for me to pick up Kennedy from camp, but I found myself driving toward Russell's house. I didn't want to be the annoying wife who didn't give him enough space, but I told myself that if I just saw that his car was there, it would give me some peace of mind. I drove up to the gate and saw that his car was in fact parked inside.

Okay, I'm just going to leave him alone, I thought. *Maybe he's got a cold or something. I don't know. Just leave the guy alone.*

I picked up Kennedy from camp, took her home, and got her settled. We planned to go out for dinner a little later. This whole time, I was still calling and texting friends, but no one had heard from Russell for several days. Even though I had seen his car, I couldn't help but worry.

Finally, I started texting with our family friend Francisco Martin, who's also one of my business partners.

"I'm just getting worried," I wrote. "I haven't heard from him."

Julie and I took Kennedy to the Coral Tree Café in Brentwood and tried to make the dinner fun for my daughter. Julie and I were laughing because they have a wonderful children's menu there, and we wanted to order from it, too, so we had all of this food that Kennedy loves: chicken fingers, kids' spaghetti, and mac and cheese.

"We have to get a salad or something grown-up," I said.

The mood was light at the table, but I couldn't shake my uneasiness. I gave Julie a meaningful look so she'd know not to say too much in front of Kennedy.

"I feel really weird about the fact that Russell's not getting back to me," I said.

"I can tell it's really bothering you," she said.

During dinner we played with Kennedy and did our best to enjoy ourselves, but the whole situation was weighing heavily on me.

I called Francisco, and we were trying to figure out what to do. Finally I told him that after dinner I planned to go by Russell's house again and knock on the door to see if he was home. Francisco said that he would meet us there. This reassured me because, for some reason, I worried that I wasn't going to be able to get through the gate, and I felt like I needed to have a guy there with me.

After dinner, I drove to Russell's house with Kennedy and Julie in the car. Francisco was already there when we arrived. While Julie waited in the car with Kennedy, Francisco and I walked up and rang the buzzer on the gate. Russell was living with a friend who had the upstairs portion of the building, while Russell occupied the whole downstairs. Francisco and I were buzzing and buzzing, but no one answered.

Finally Russell's friend's voice came over the intercom. I could tell that he had been asleep. I felt bad about waking him. He didn't want to come down to the gate to let us in, but I was adamant.

"This is Taylor," I said.

"Oh, okay, okay," he said.

"I need to see Russell right now," I said.

"I haven't seen him since Friday," he said.

I looked at Francisco. I didn't want to be rude, but I was starting to feel frantic. No one I knew had heard from Russell in several days.

"I need to see Russell's face right now," I said.

I just felt in my heart that something was wrong, and I was getting so wound up that Francisco and I were talking about trying to jump the gate. Finally, Russell's friend came down from the house and opened the gate for us. I questioned him as we walked up toward the house together. What he told me made me go into complete panic mode.

"Russell's door has been locked since Friday night," he said.

It was now Monday evening.

"What the fuck is wrong with you?" I said. "Somebody has had his door locked since Friday, and you haven't busted it down?"

"I looked in the window and no one was there," he said.

I tried to calm myself. I knew that it was possible to see through Russell's bathroom window into the bedroom. And I knew that men were much more private than women, and it might not be unusual for them not to communicate with or check on each other all weekend. But by this point I was not going to feel better until I saw Russell.

"I don't care," I said. "Take me to his room."

The three of us walked up to the house and past Russell's

silver Mercedes. Russell's friend pried the bathroom window open and climbed in while Francisco and I waited outside. My heart was pounding and I could hardly breathe.

"See, no one's in here," Russell's friend said from within the house.

"Keep looking," I called. "Keep looking."

Somehow, I knew right then that Russell *was* in there, and that something was wrong. I just knew it. We were connected; he really was like family to me. On top of that, all of the circumstances of the day were so uncharacteristic for Russell, whom I knew so well. He never missed a day of work. In the nearly six years we'd been together, I'd only known him to not go into the office on maybe two workdays. It was his favorite pastime in the world. He was attached to his BlackBerry like nobody I'd ever met in my life. For that phone not to be on all day Monday was beyond a reasonable explanation.

As soon as Russell's friend turned the corner into the bedroom, he began to scream.

"Oh, my God, he's hung himself!" he yelled.

He ran back into the bathroom and frantically scrambled through the window to get outside and away from the body. Nothing made sense anymore. Everything was pain and loss and terror. I ran into the road, with Francisco close behind me, fell down onto the asphalt in the middle of the street, and began to scream. And then I had a thought that made me feel worse than ever.

My little girl is out there in the car.

Julie later told me that when Kennedy heard me screaming she turned to her.

"Did my daddy do something dumb?" Kennedy asked.

"I don't know," Julie said. "Mommy's going to tell you later."

As I kneeled in the street, it hit me all at once that my little girl had lost her daddy. That I had lost Russell. That he was gone. I knew I had to pull myself together for Kennedy, but my emotions were beyond my control. Francisco helped me to my feet and held me in his arms. I tried to stop screaming, but I couldn't.

Meanwhile, Francisco had called 911 and was getting them to dispatch an ambulance, while I screamed in the background. I needed to talk to Dr. Sophy right away. I needed someone to help me make sense of what had happened.

Finally I didn't have any screams left and I grew silent.

How am I going to get my daughter out of here before they pull her daddy's body out of this house? I thought.

———

MINUTES LATER, EMERGENCY VEHICLES and police officers appeared on the scene. I made them swear to me that they would not remove Russell's sheet-clad body while Kennedy was there. At first I didn't want to see him in this way, either.

"Please don't pull my husband's body out with a sheet over him because I can't see him," I said. "I can't see him."

But then it sunk in that I would never see Russell again. I wanted desperately to touch him, to hold him. But they wouldn't let me.

My biggest concern was that we get Kennedy away from

there before the paparazzi descended on the house, as I feared they would at any moment. The emergency vehicles had blocked the driveway, so we couldn't get my car out onto the street until after they had left. Julie and I walked Kennedy down past the emergency vehicles. Luckily, just then, one of the neighbors drove up and offered to take them down the hill, where Gloria was waiting for them. Thankfully, no paparazzi were there to capture my despair or further scare my daughter.

While Francisco and I waited for the Los Angeles coroner, who had been summoned by the detectives, Francisco's wife, my mother, and several of my friends arrived. They had brought me water and protein bars, but of course I couldn't eat anything. All I could do was cry. I cried in the street. I cried in my friends' cars. Hours passed, and still the coroner had not arrived. Thankfully, the paparazzi had not materialized yet, either.

Finally, five hours later, the coroner still had not arrived. I'm still not sure what took him so long, but the emergency workers told me to go home. I was exhausted and distraught and incredibly grateful that the paparazzi had never come.

My mother drove me home, but I didn't sleep at all that night. I just lay awake in bed and thought about the last moments of Russell's life, even though I tried to avoid the images that rose in my mind. I hated so much to think of him all alone, despondent, scared. I wished desperately that he had called me, had let me help him. I cried and I cried.

The next morning, the phone started ringing early, and it didn't stop. I couldn't bear the thought of facing anyone. I didn't know what I would tell Kennedy, or how. And I couldn't imagine making a statement, planning the service, and whatever came next. All I could think of was Russell and that I wanted him back. Thankfully, when I opened my eyes that morning, one of my friends who works in media training was standing above my bed.

"You can fall to pieces today," she said. "You can stay in this bed all day. I'm going to manage the press."

I was so relieved when I heard this; it was really the best gift that anyone could have given me at that moment. I was in shock and had no words. She literally went outside onto my doorstep, where swarms of paparazzi were now camped, and handled everything for me.

The media frenzy surrounding Russell's death made it incredibly difficult for me to mourn. Every morning, I woke up to the phone ringing. It was my attorney, my manager, my publicist, someone calling me for me to deal with an issue straight out of bed, and it continued in this fashion for the first week or two.

My BlackBerry was filled with text messages and missed phone calls from people who wanted me to call them back. I was grateful for their messages, and for the flowers and food that friends sent to the house, but I was totally overwhelmed. I couldn't talk about my loss yet, and I wasn't prepared to handle others' grief or mourn with them. The housewives were incredibly thoughtful during this time, which I appreciated. I knew they were probably feeling many emotions themselves because of all of our interactions throughout the year regarding the violence in my marriage, so I appreciated their loyal support.

From the time when I came home after we found Russell's

body, I didn't leave my house for a week, until it was time to go to Forest Lawn to plan Russell's cremation and service. The house was still surrounded by a number of paparazzi, so I was incredibly tense as I got ready to go out into the world that day. I was upset enough about the decisions I faced that morning, and the emotions they would bring up, without having to deal with all of this, too.

With my Escalade parked in the garage, a bodyguard who had been sent over by a friend for a few days to protect Kennedy and me from the paparazzi onslaught and because early rumors that Russell had been murdered had not yet been dismissed, put down a blanket in the back of the car for me to lie on. He then covered me with a black blanket. Then, with my bodyguard driving and Julie in the passenger seat, he pulled out into the street. As we drove away, the paparazzi started to follow us. They were surrounding the car and pursuing us so aggressively that my bodyguard had to constantly change lanes, and we almost got into several accidents. The photographers followed us through the gates of Forest Lawn and pulled in front of the Escalade on several occasions. They clearly wanted to block us off, so we would have to stop and they could come up to the car and take pictures. We wound around and around and around the long, windy roads that pass through the cemetery. The whole time, we kept calling the administrative offices at Forest Lawn because they had told us they would help us with security, but no one was coming to our aid.

Finally we went around to the morgue entrance, where a cemetery employee opened up two large double doors so we could back the Escalade into the building. The paparazzi had already gotten out of their cars and were rushing up to us with their cameras drawn, so my bodyguard quickly grabbed me, wrapped me up in the blanket, and threw me over his shoulder. As he did, my shoes fell off, so I was barefoot. He carried me through the morgue entrance, just like that.

Once we were inside, planning the service, I suddenly started shaking my head and laughing a bit in the middle of the meeting. Everyone else was staring at me like I had lost my mind, but I had just been struck by a funny thought: anyone who had seen my bodyguard carrying me over his shoulder into the morgue, wrapped in a blanket with my feet bare, must have thought he was carrying a dead body. I imagined some nice, normal family who was there at Forest Lawn that day to plan a service seeing this scene and thinking, *good grief, this place is so unprofessional*. In the midst of that much stress and sadness, it felt good to laugh for a moment.

When the meeting was over, I went out the same way I had come in. After we had planned Russell's service, I was supposed to choose a place for his ashes to be interned, but the paparazzi were following us so closely that we couldn't look at any of the possible locations.

The next morning, I sneaked out of the house at 7:00 a.m. to go back to Forest Lawn and choose the place to intern Russell's ashes. But again, the paparazzi were on us so unrelentingly that I wasn't able to make the trip. All I wanted was to be able to plan a really nice service to celebrate Russell's life, but the constant paparazzi scrutiny made even the smallest task a complicated endeavor during the days after his death.

Russell's family told me that they wanted to hold a service for him in Texas and asked me to send a portion of his ashes to be buried there. I was happy to oblige. But Russell had spent nearly two decades of his life in Los Angeles, and he had so many friends and business associates there—not to mention that two of his three children lived in the city—so I wanted to hold a service to celebrate Russell's life in the place that had been his home for so long.

Because I was determined that the service really would be a celebration of Russell, rather than a somber affair, I hired a celebrant instead of a preacher or minister. She came over to my house and spent time with me in preparation to speak about Russell. She asked me questions about what he had been like and what he had enjoyed. I told her things that I wanted her to share with others; how, when he wanted to get things going, he always used to say, "Let's go," or "Let's rock 'n' roll." That he was from Texas but had gone to the University of Hawaii and had a lifelong love for Hawaii. That he liked barbecue. And, of course, that he loved his children very much and was so incredibly proud of them. I told her how he always used to say how beautiful Kennedy was and how he bragged about how good his boys were at sports; how Aiden was a great baseball player and Griffin wanted to be just like him. I also told her a few stories, such as the anecdote about how Russell had given me the necklace at our wedding, which showed his more sensitive side.

I gathered photos and gave them to a friend who created a DVD featuring a montage for the service of all of the important people in Russell's life. It featured lots of pictures of Russell with his kids at all different ages, and him with his mom and dad, his grandma, his sister, and his nephews; Russell and I together throughout our marriage; big groups of our friends.

My friend Josh Tatum, who is a singer/songwriter, came over before the service with the bones of a song that was perfect for the occasion. He and I spent several nights in my backyard working on the lyrics until we had basically written a song for Russell's service, which was a really wonderful healing process for me. I also asked my good friend Linda Thompson if any of her songs might be appropriate for the service. There was a song she had written for Josh Groban that was just right, so she gave it to Josh Tatum to learn. We really took great care with the song selection for that day and finally chose a third song for Josh to play as well. Josh's involvement meant a great deal to me because he was really there for me in the days after Russell's death, so I appreciated the fact that he was able to sing at Russell's service.

One of the hardest decisions about the service was deciding if Kennedy should attend. At first I thought I would have her go. She knew that her daddy was dead, and I thought that it might be healing for her to be part of the service. But then I began to reconsider. Many of the people who came by the house following Russell's death were incredibly upset, and I could tell that it was hard for Kennedy to be around such intense emotion. I was afraid that she might see some people in really significant despair at the service.

I also wasn't sure how I would explain to her the fact that her father had been cremated. We had decided to have his cremated remains in a box there for people to pay their respects to if they wanted. Kennedy didn't know about cremation, and I was afraid that it would confuse her that her daddy could fit in that little box. And I worried that it would be scary for her if I had to explain that he had been burned. I also didn't know how intense the media frenzy would be that day, so I decided it would be best for her to stay home. I discussed my decision with Dr. Sophy, and he agreed that it was the best way to handle a difficult situation.

Telling Kennedy that her daddy had died was hard enough. I was glad to have the support of Dr. Sophy and the child psychiatrist I had found for Kennedy, but no matter how many helpful tools they equipped me with, I still had to sit down with her and deliver the impossible news.

"Daddy got sick, and Daddy died," I said.

It's hard to know how much children understand or how they conceptualize an idea as big as death, but she seemed to comprehend this news and begin to cope with it. But I hadn't counted on the logic of the five-year-old mind. A few days later, she came to me with questions.

"Well, Mommy, what if you get sick and you die?" she asked. "And then, my grandma and grandpa get sick, and they die? And what if Julie dies? And what if Jax dies?"

My heart broke for her. In her mind, she had worked out a scenario where everyone in her life—including the dog, Jax—died and she was left all alone. I knew that I had to be more specific about what had happened to her daddy to quiet her anxiety. At her age, getting sick meant having a cold, and I didn't want her to be frightened that anytime she or other

people in her life had a col⌐
me and tried to explain.

"Daddy was sick in the he⌐
kind of sick than when you and I ⌐

That seemed to put her fears to ⌐
to watch her closely and talk to her abo⌐
possible, and read her books about the ⌐
make sure she's getting all of the support she⌐
counselors wanted me to tell her that her dac⌐
suicide, but I've decided that she's too young. She ⌐
know that it's possible for people to end their own li⌐
think that the whole explanation involved would only c⌐
her. I can imagine how her questions would go.

"Your daddy took his own life," I would say.

"Took it where?" she would ask.

It has been a difficult decision and one that I reassess constantly. But like so much that I am facing right now, I just have to trust that I know what's best for my daughter and that we will get through this.

I told Kennedy after Russell died that we could pick a star in the sky to represent her daddy, and that we can talk to him anytime she has something to say. She picked what she described as the "middle" star, and we often look up at her special star so she can talk to her daddy.

"I miss you, Daddy," she says. "I wish you weren't dead."

At the same time, Kennedy's feelings about Russell are almost as complicated as mine are, and not all of her memories are positive. She frequently mentions the two instances

ssell yelled at me in front of her. I continue to do my
try to explain.

at's why Mommy and Daddy couldn't live in the same
e anymore," I say. "Because that's not okay."

hope that she also will remember that Russell and I sepa-
ed soon after he yelled at me, and that she'll always make
e connection that her mommy was strong enough to stand
up for herself.

It's a complicated challenge for me because Kennedy saw
Russell be verbally abusive to me in a fairly intense way. And
while I want her to cherish Russell's memory, I don't want her
to think that those behaviors were acceptable. I absolutely
don't want her to go out and one day replicate those patterns
in her own romantic life.

Thankfully, she has also made some statements that make
me think that maybe she has gotten the message. One morning, we were lying in bed together and she turned and looked
at me.

"Mommy, you're going to get married again," she said. "And
he's going to be nice to you because my daddy used to scream
at you a lot."

Oh, my God, I thought.

At the same time that it was hard for me to hear Kennedy's
unpleasant memories of Russell, I was so happy that she had
already made the distinction in her mind between a good marriage and a bad one. Because she was so young when Russell
died, I hope that the memories of those unhappy times will
fade and that she can mostly remember the wonderful experiences she did have with her dad.

chapter thirteen

Picking Up the Pieces

As I put on a black dress the morning of Russell's service, it all seemed impossible and surreal.

Today I'm a widow, I thought.

I felt way too young to be a widow, and Russell was too young to be dead. I kept finding myself wondering if he really was dead. It didn't seem possible that all of this could be happening. As I got ready, I prepared myself for another day of trying to come to terms with the tragedy of Russell's suicide while attempting to outrun the paparazzi.

Once again I had to climb onto the floor in the back of the Escalade and pull a blanket over my head to avoid being photographed. All day I never felt like I was getting a chance to celebrate Russell's life as I wanted because I kept having to attend to details such as the security we had hired to make sure only invited guests gained entry. Instead of being able to mingle and hug all of the guests and spend time with them, I had to come in last after everyone had already been seated and leave first, to dodge the media frenzy.

I had asked Francisco to speak at the service, and both he and our friend Shelly, who had asked to say a few words, spoke very movingly about Russell and what he had meant to them. The celebrant did a wonderful job and kept the mood as light as possible while also acknowledging our loss. I wanted to share some thoughts with those who had gathered, so I told the story about Russell giving me my necklace at our wedding and tried to honor that side of his personality.

"I know that most of you only knew the business side of Russell, and the serious side of him, but he had a sensitive side, too," I said. "And he loved his children, and he was so proud of them."

It all seemed to go by so quickly, and then it was over.

And then I broke down.

I had taken an indefinite hiatus from the show since Russell's death, and in the wake of his service, I was in no condition to go back in front of the cameras. I was paralyzed. I couldn't sleep. I couldn't talk to anyone. I couldn't even function. I sat out on the patio behind my house by the pool for weeks. My mom, Julie, and Gloria took care of Kennedy's basic needs, and when she was in the house, I tried to pull it together for her so I wouldn't upset her even more. But the rest of the time, I fell apart. My phone was full of texts and messages from friends who wanted me to call them back, but conversation was difficult for me.

Every person I spoke with seemed to say the same things:

"How did this happen?"

"Why did he do this?"

I don't know why, I thought. *I have no idea.*

As much as I loved my friends and was grateful for their presence, I couldn't face the discussions they needed me to have. And yet I felt a great deal of guilt about not being able to call them back. I talked to Dr. Sophy about the situation and he explained that my friends needed to connect with me as a way to ease their own pain about the abuse I had suffered and Russell's death. I understood what he was saying and was sympathetic, but the thought was just too much. I isolated myself as a protective mechanism to survive the aftermath of my loss.

So many of the friends I did talk to, even briefly, told me that when they first heard about Russell's death, they were certain it was going to be followed by the report that my body and Kennedy's body also had been found. My friend Jennifer told me that when she heard the news report on her car radio at 7:00 a.m. the morning after Russell's body was discovered, she had to pull her car over because she was so certain she was about to hear news of my death, too.

I felt very grateful to be alive. The statistics suggest that many domestic abusers who choose to end their own lives also take out their victims at the same time. I also thought back to the many times Russell had said that he was afraid he was going to kill me someday. At the time I hadn't realized just how much of a possibility that had really been. But now that I knew that Russell had been unstable enough to take his own life, I recognized that he absolutely could have taken my life as well.

Russell's suicide made me finally face the extent of the mental illness he was struggling with throughout our marriage.

Clearly he was not of sound mind and body. Dr. Sophy was extremely helpful to me in processing all of this. He told me that Russell had gone far too long without treatment. It was true.

I had even more sympathy for Russell, now that I understood all that he was up against. He felt like he had to control everyone because he couldn't let his guard down and trust people after all of the horrible, violent behavior he had been exposed to in his youth. The fact that this same violence had come out in him seemed more like an illness than anything else, something that required more substantial treatment than just prosecution or anger management classes. Not to mention the delusions that afflicted him due to the chemical imbalances in his brain. As hard as it has been to let Russell go, I finally had to agree with Dr. Sophy when he said that because Russell was struggling against so many terrible demons every day, we should view the end of Russell's life as the end of his suffering.

While Russell was at peace, my life was becoming more difficult by the day, as I realized how much Russell had misled me about the state of his finances and the amount of trouble that was bearing down on him at the time of his death.

From the early days of our marriage, Russell had intertwined our finances in a complicated way. Because he had just filed for bankruptcy and I had a credit rating of 800 at the time, he had put all the bills in my name. But because he was so paranoid that I might be trying to use him for his money, and, I now suspect, because he was trying to outrun so many potentially damning secrets about his business life, he did not allow me to know anything about the details of our financial life or even the documents he was having me sign. It soon became clear that I may be responsible for many of Russell's business dealings that I had little or no knowledge of, or that he had forced me to sign documents without any understanding of what I was getting involved in.

Soon after Russell died, I realized that, as his widow, I was now viewed by some people as responsible for his legal woes, even though I was left in the dark on what he did in business and how he made money to support the family. Not least of this was a $1.5-million-dollar lawsuit Russell faced, which has named me directly. The case goes back to the medical records portal and another company that Russell formed before we ever met. Early in our relationship, he apparently had a falling-out with his business partner, who sued Russell when they severed ties. To settle the disagreement, Russell had to agree to a number of stipulations. These included identifying all shareholders at both companies, as well as their contact information. In the event he missed an investor's name the settlement agreement required Russell to pay $1 million for the first missed name and $250,000 for each missed name thereafter. When Russell went in to negotiate and sign this agreement, the ex-business partner said he wanted me to sign as well, so that if there was the need for a settlement, Russell couldn't just shift his assets into my name and claim he didn't have enough funds to settle. Russell also involved Kennedy, who was one at the time, saying that if there were any funds left in a trust for Kennedy, they could go after that trust. The thought of this potential danger filled me with dread, but I was living in a position of such inequality in my marriage at that time that I had no choice but to keep my mouth shut and sign.

Russell threatened to beat me if I didn't sign. Based on his prior physical abuse to me, I had no choice but to sign the agreement I was given. So I did. And I certainly wasn't at a place in my relationship with Russell where I would have confronted, or even questioned, him or his advisers and attorneys about any of this.

Well, not long after Russell and I separated, these men decided to come after Russell. And after he died, they decided to come after me. As I recall, the attorney Russell hired regarding the settlement of Russell's problem charged $50,000 in fees. That's just one of many business disputes I'm facing, so I could end up with millions of dollars in legal bills. And that's a lot to think about when I'm trying to provide for a little girl.

And those are only the problems I know about. From the moment I met Russell, he carried a locked briefcase that contained all of his banking records, checkbooks, and papers. After he died, I made some alarming discoveries. When I got Russell's things back from the coroner, his wallet contained ten debit cards; he had accounts at ten different banks. All of the accounts were empty. There was no $14 million trust. In fact, there was no money at all, and he faced $200,000 in debt for the month of August alone. Russell was in such dire financial straits at the time he died that he had pawned his Rolex Concord for $9,000. When his body was found, it also was discovered that he had left a little more than $7,000 in cash on his nightstand with a $25,000 bill for his son Griffin's private school. No suicide note was ever found.

Every day I have a conversation with someone about the legal ramifications of what I've been left with, and it's scary to think that more problems will probably reveal themselves in the future. Because of the nature of Russell's business, he had financial dealings with *hundreds* of people, and I'm the one who's been left responsible for all of that now.

It wasn't only the reality of Russell's bleak monetary situation that was news to me. When I was going through his papers, I found a bunch of documents that both saddened me and gave me a sense of validation, including court documents that had been filed by his ex-wife. The information they contained was chilling. It detailed exactly the same kind of paranoia, bullying, and violence, years before I had met him that Russell had subjected me to. She, too, had been a victim of Russell's threats and verbal and physical attacks. She, too, had seen his drinking aggravate his aggressive behavior. And yet I had known nothing about any of this, except for the sanitized version of events that Russell had chosen to tell me.

On top of the shock of these revelations, the media attention has never completely subsided, so I've been forced to relive the more grisly aspects of Russell's suicide nearly every day. In the weeks after his death, it seemed like I woke up every day to something in the news that I didn't want to hear.

First, it was the release of the 911 call, which immediately made me worry about the fact that it's going to be in the public domain forever, and that my daughter is inevitably going to hear it someday. I didn't listen to it for a long time, and then one day when I was interviewed at the house, they played it between segments. I didn't feel up for watching the interview right away when it aired, but when I finally did, I didn't fast-forward through the 911 call. I wanted to listen, even though it was hard for me to hear, especially the part where they talked about Russell's daughter being there, because it brought me back so vividly to just how horrible and painful that night had been.

Then the coroner called to tell me that he had completed his report, and they wanted to give me a copy before he released it to the press. He offered to bring a copy to my house before it went public. But I knew better than that. When he had come to question me about Russell's death, an especially large number of paparazzi came with him and waited outside while we were talking. He assured me that he was not going to talk to the press. And then he went outside and essentially held a press conference and photo opportunity from my front steps. I told him that I would prefer it if he just faxed the report to me.

As soon as the report came in over the fax that day, I started to read it, but it was too upsetting, and I couldn't finish. Finally, later that night, when everyone else was in bed, I sat down by myself and read through the whole thing. Even though it was hard for me to face the specifics of Russell's last moments and death, I had spent so many nights lying awake wondering about all of these very details that I needed to know for sure what had happened and how. I've always had regrets that I didn't get to see him one last time, so I needed to read the report, because it was the closest I was going to get to having that final moment with him.

The most surprising—and hardest—detail for me was the

fact that there were no alcohol or drugs in Russell's system at the time of his death. I wanted to believe that his suicide was just a bad, irrational decision he had made in a drunken stupor. But the other significant aspect of this detail was that he stopped taking his medication about a week before his death. He had brought his prescription to be refilled and was supposed to pick it up on the Thursday before his death, but he never did. Of course, that fact just reiterated the severity of Russell's mental illness, and that if he wasn't able to face up to that illness, and commit himself to getting the treatment he needed for it, then there was nothing the rest of us could have done to save him. While it was comforting for me to learn all this, I couldn't understand why the information was released to the public as it was. But I've since had to let go of my anger about all of that.

Through all of this, my number one priority was trying to keep myself and the household together enough so there would be a feeling of normalcy and safety for Kennedy.

I had so many powerful and conflicting emotions about Russell every day that sometimes I felt like *I* was going crazy. I was still dealing with the emotional aftermath of the abuse, and I couldn't just forget or deny all of the unacceptable behavior Russell had exhibited toward me.

Sometimes when I went into our bedroom, I would find myself looking behind me, even though I knew he was gone, because he had so conditioned me to fear the possibility that he could attack me at any time.

I've also felt angry at him for not being able to get the help he needed so he could stay with his family, and for leaving me with such a financial mess. It's hard for me to accept that he wasn't able to remain to see Kennedy's hair grow long, or to walk her down the aisle. But of course, I know that he was facing a level of despair so deep that he could no longer take responsibility for others, even his daughter. He had to go.

On the other hand, I still loved him until the end, and I would have stayed with him forever if he could have gotten his violent temper under control. I've missed him incredibly since he's been gone. And I know that he loved me, too. In the days since he died, I've pulled down the beautiful photo albums he gave me for Christmas and looked through the photos so many times. They remind me of the many wonderful moments we shared in our relationship, including so many happy days with our daughter, all the trips we took, and the fun times we had with all three kids. But sometimes the memories are just too painful.

It also was difficult to come to terms with the fact that there was no more hope of healing or reconciliation. This has left me with a feeling of tremendous guilt. We were supposed to be a family, so it's very hard for me to accept that Russell didn't call me and give me the opportunity to help him. I had saved him from getting in trouble so many times before, and I kept thinking that if he had only let me know that he needed me, I would have been there for him. I even felt guilty that maybe, if I had sent him to jail at some point earlier in our marriage, he would have gotten more aggressive treatment, and he would be alive today. I have infinite what-ifs and regrets.

At the same time, I've had to rebuild my life. When Russell died, the producers of the show and everyone at Bravo were incredibly thoughtful and kind. They told me to take off as much time as I needed. After a two-month break from the show, I finally felt ready to go back in front of the cameras, and in mid-October we filmed a postscript to the season two finale for the show. We had filmed the finale back in July, following my eye surgery, at which time I had taken several weeks off from the show, as we were coming close to wrapping up the second season. After my swelling and bruising had subsided, I rejoined my castmates for the finale—and although I was wearing a great deal of makeup, the injury was still visible. Dr. Sophy accompanied me to the taping of that episode, during which I made amends to all of the girls for the way my relationship with Russell had impacted their lives and my friendships with them.

Of course, I had seen all the girls during this break. Many of them attended Russell's service, and they all reached out to me in their own ways to offer their support and friendship. But it still felt very emotional to be officially reunited with them. When I had signed up to do the show, I had hoped it would either positively impact my marriage or give me an escape. I hadn't counted on the fact that I would form intense friendships that would force me to grow and reevaluate myself and my marriage. Or that they would help me to find the confidence and self-esteem I had lacked my entire life. It was wonderful to see everyone, publicly thank them for their support, and to have a chance to catch up on all that had happened in their lives during the time I had been away from the show.

Now that my lifelong fear has come true, and I am a single mom, I'm finding that it's not as bad as I had worried. I'm much stronger than I ever gave myself credit for, and I'm capable of doing so much more for myself and my daughter than I ever knew. At the same time, being in the public eye as I am, and given the number of sensitive decisions that have had to be made following Russell's death, I've had to rely on a number of advisers. And I've found that my old personality traits have made these relationships very difficult. Just at the time in my life when I had finally stood up to Russell and was trying to become an independent woman, I found that I was allowing people in my business life to take away my power and control me, just as I had always allowed my boyfriends and husband to do. All of my old difficulties of drawing and enforcing healthy boundaries because of my fear of being abandoned came up again, making it even harder for me to have the confidence to stand up for myself. And I found myself agreeing to things I didn't want to do, and growing resentful and passive-aggressive as a result. It made what was already a difficult, emotionally draining time even more challenging. These old patterns also have resurfaced in my friendships, and it's been tempting for me to retreat rather than face all of this.

I've finally been forced to learn that I can just be me, and feel like if someone doesn't like me, it's okay. Yes, it's embarrassing that I'm forty years old, and I'm just now figuring this out. But that's how long it took.

Luckily, I have Dr. Sophy in my life, and he has been a tremendous source of support. As he has explained to me, while most people don't like to be controlled, I find some comfort in it because I didn't grow and mature as I should have when I was younger. But by doing that work now, he is helping me to identify these patterns early on and actually confront people in my life rather than just running away.

As I have said, there have been times when it's been difficult for me to admit just how severe my emotional issues were and how long it has taken me to overcome them. I am well aware that there are many people whose childhoods were much worse than mine. I had so much to be thankful for—a loving mom and grandparents, food on the table, the opportunity to go to school and gain an education that prepared me to have a career as an adult. But that's why I think it's so important to be honest about all these issues, and to remove the accompanying shame, so that others who travel this same path can feel supported in the work they need to do. It can be a little bit daunting to realize that I'm still facing challenges at my age that most people mastered decades ago, but I am learning. And not just for me. I'm constantly aware of trying to model healthy behavior for Kennedy so that she grows up with all of the tools she needs to be a strong, independent woman who has loving, equal relationships.

Grief is complicated, especially following the loss of a relationship as complex as the one I had with Russell, and given the fact that he committed suicide. I've tried to read several books on the subject, but I haven't been able to focus long enough to get through them. Luckily, I've had such wonderful support from my family and friends, Dr. Sophy, and everyone at Bravo. And sometimes it has been the most surprising moments that have fortified me and given me the strength to go on.

After Russell had been dead for about five weeks, which

I had mostly spent crying alone at home, one of my friends invited a girlfriend and me over for dinner at his house. He's kind of a tough guy, but he loves to cook, so he got us set up with wineglasses at the island in his kitchen and set to work on our meal. While he prepared dinner, he gave me a much-needed pep talk with just the right amount of tough love to snap me out of my grief and give me a sense of purpose.

"Listen, you can wallow in this for the rest of your life, destroy your life, and destroy Kennedy's life," he said. "Or you can put on your big-girl pants and go out there and do something about it."

He's right, I thought. *I have to live for the living now. I don't have any more options for helping Russell, and I can't fix our relationship. I couldn't fix it when he was alive. Now I can only clean up the mess he's left behind, and live a life for my daughter and me.*

As simple as that sounds, it changed everything. Everyone else had been coddling me, crying with me, and sending me flowers. Of course, I'd needed that sympathy, too, especially in the first weeks after Russell's death. But this friend was right; now that I'd taken the time to mourn my husband, it was time to do something to help myself and others.

It was such a relief, in a way, to receive permission to move on. I had been consumed with questions about how long it was normal to feel as bad as I did, when I was allowed to laugh again—if I ever felt like laughing again, which seemed impossible for a long time—and when people would want to be around me, not to help me get through this tough time, but because they wanted to spend time with *me*.

I felt like such a black widow in the wake of Russell's death. When I did first start venturing out, I could literally see people pointing at me and putting their hands up to their mouths to try to block the fact that they were talking about me.

I can see you, I thought. *I know you're talking about me.*

At first this was really hard for me to face. As someone who's always been incredibly insecure, and feared the judgment of others, it was like some kind of nightmare was coming true in real life. But as with everything else, I've been working through it, and the experience is making me stronger in ways I never believed possible. I made the choice to be on *The Real Housewives,* and it has given me so much and enriched my life in so many ways, so I am learning to make peace with all aspects of the publicity and notoriety that come with that.

As soon as I began to make a plan for the next stage of my life, I focused on one of my central passions: advocacy and education around the issue of domestic violence. I have continued to volunteer at the 1736 Family Crisis Center since I made my first shelter visit back in 2005, and they did so much more to keep me on my feet during the worst days of my marriage than they ever could know. I have been so thrilled that *Housewives* has given me such a high-profile platform for spotlighting all the amazing work they do. And now I have the opportunity to help even more women around the world.

One of the biggest problems surrounding domestic violence is the shame and the secrecy that too often allow it to go unaddressed until it's too late. So many people have approached me to say that they had no idea I was being abused, and that when the news broke they couldn't believe it was true. We have to support women to start speaking up. Domestic violence is not like cancer, where people feel inspired to rally around and fight toward health together. But I believe it should be. The shame I felt as a little girl because of the abuse in my home kept me from talking about that abuse and made it possible for me to grow up from a little girl who kept my abused mom's secret into an abused woman with painful secrets of my own.

I have a tremendous amount of guilt that I was not able to break this cycle of violence before Kennedy witnessed Russell's verbal assaults on me, and that I put her in danger of repeating the cycle in her own life. So I am doing what I can now: getting her the best help I can, so she has a place to talk about her response to what happened and so she can be supported to grow up into a strong, healthy woman who will make better choices than I did.

I also want to speak directly to other women who have come from upbringings where there has been violence and make them aware of the potential for repeating the pattern, and tell them that they deserve more and have other options beyond falling into the same painful pattern themselves. My goal is to stop the abuse before it starts, to reach young women at high schools and colleges. I want to address those who are just like I was at that age, insecure, and vulnerable to giving away their power to men because of their low self-esteem. I want to share with them some of the red flags in the relationships I had, which I was not able to see at the time, but which can hopefully help them to avoid the same mistakes I made.

Pursuing a man or a relationship at all costs is not healthy.

If someone does not want to be with you, that does not mean you're not worthy of having a great relationship; it just means it's not a good fit with that particular guy. Even if you can convince him to be with you, as I did with my fiancé and husband, there is already such an imbalance of power from the beginning that it will be nearly impossible to form an equal relationship that is respectful on both sides.

It can actually be a good thing not to have a boyfriend; being alone allows time for personal reflection and growth. And there's no need to rush from one relationship into another, especially because doing so usually entails choosing to be with people who aren't really a good fit, just to have someone.

Finally, for the first time in my life, I can give this advice, not just as someone who is parroting what I have read in self-help books or what Dr. Sophy has told me, but from my own very-hard-won experience. I don't need a man to complete me or to make me happy. I've always felt like I needed someone to run to my rescue, but now I realize that I'm the adult, the one who's doing the rescuing—for my daughter, for me, and for the other abused women I am able to help.

I know I was supposed to be learning this kind of self-confidence all along, but I got my lesson compacted into one incredibly difficult, but ultimately important, six-year relationship, plus the time it has taken me to recover since then. I don't have the option of retreating anymore or letting someone else take over my life. I have to learn how to manage my own conflict. I have to meet with people who intimidate me and make decisions that scare me. I have to learn how to sleep alone in the house. And every night that I do sleep alone, and every overwhelming moment I do master, give me that much more self-confidence and make the process of rebuilding that much easier.

And now that I've hopefully gotten through the worst of the surprises and started to face up to the most overwhelming messes since Russell died, I'm able to start thinking about what I want for my daughter and me. As I said, I don't want a man right now. But I do know that, should I love again, it will have to be a different kind of love—a grown-up partnership, as opposed to the unhealthy, obsessive love that Russell and I shared.

I'm rebuilding in other areas as well. I really regret that I've had so few strong female relationships in my life because I always put so much emphasis on my need to have a man in my life, and on the validation that I got from these men. I feel so incredibly blessed that I was given five strong, outspoken, dynamic female friends in the form of the other Housewives at just the time I needed their friendship more than ever in my life. I hope to strengthen those relationships even more. I also feel so incredibly grateful for the handful of significant friends—including Dwight and Jennifer—who really have stuck with me through the worst days of my life, moments so much more dramatic than anything that played out in front of the cameras. I only hope that I can repay them for their kindness, patience, and love during the years to come. And I plan to make even more good friends, the kind I open up to and use my voice with, even if it means going out on a limb and telling them where I actually want to go for dinner.

I want to be a normal person again—to hear about my

friends' lives, to discuss something other than what they've read about me in the tabloids, and to let things quiet down and settle into a normal life with my daughter. I feel so grateful that I got that big life I always dreamed of, but maybe it doesn't have to be quite so big.

Finally, I feel that if I can use my public platform for good in the area of domestic abuse education and advocacy, then it will all have been worth it. My main goal is that one day my daughter will look back and say, "My mom had her own problems, and she made a lot of bad choices, but in the end, she did everything she could to help other people."

Epilogue

Here I sit in Vail, Colorado, the same place where I had a nervous breakdown on camera just a few months ago. It has been three months since I discovered my husband's body following his suicide. My biggest fears have come true.

I am alone.

I am surrounded by attorneys.

I am learning terms like "probate."

I am discovering all of the unexpected and painful pitfalls following the death of a loved one; the questions of what to do with his socks, and his leased car, which can't be returned because it's in my name, and yet I can't bring myself to drive.

I am cleaning up Russell's colossal mess: failed businesses, angry investors, lawsuits.

It's everything that a conflict avoider like me most fears.

But surprisingly, it's not so bad.

Everything in my life has become much clearer for me now. The sun is brighter. I really pay attention to birds in the trees, the clouds covering the Gore Range. I see the real value in everything that surrounds me and in my life. My little girl's laugh is worth so much more to me than anything on Rodeo Drive.

There are no Housewives from the program with me in Vail. No paparazzi. Just me, the mountain, and friends; as I get down to rebuilding myself and my life, and learning to love Shana. The bubble of control Russell placed over our lives has burst, and I finally feel comfortable with myself.

Not that it's been easy to let go. Sometimes I sit in our closet and hold the last shirt he ever wore. I can smell Russell in the fabric, and I miss him terribly. Then there are times when I round a corner in my home and I feel terrified, as if he is going to jump out at me. It confuses me that I can love and fear him equally. But I still do.

Sitting here in breathtaking Vail, finishing my book, I feel more alive than ever. But I find myself wondering how I got here, how I could have missed every warning sign along the road. I know it was my insecurities, and my own demons, that made me drive too fast and run all the stop signs in my desperate attempt to bind myself to Russell so he would make everything okay for me. I've since learned the hard way that I'm the only one who can do this. And now I want to give back by helping other women to read the signs along the path to abusive relationships, to avoid the dangers and difficulties I withstood. I have a mission: for the rest of my life, I am committed to identifying the dangers for others and leaving a legacy for Kennedy that she can be proud of. The cycle of violence stops with me.

Domestic Violence Resource Guide

If you are in immediate danger, call 911

National Domestic Violence 24-hour hotline: 1-800-799-SAFE (7233); TTY, 1-800-787-3224

National Online Resource Center on Violence Against Women: www.vawnet.org

National Resource Center on Domestic Violence: 1-800-537-2238; www.nrcdv.org

1736 Family Crisis Center hotlines—California numbers—will accept collect calls: 1-310-379-3620; 1-310-370-5902; 1-213-745-6434;1-213-222-1237;1-562-388-7652;www.1736 familycrisiscenter.org

National Resource Centers

National Center on Domestic Violence, Trauma, and Mental Health: 1-312-726-7020; www.nationalcenterdvtraumamh.org

National Network to End Domestic Violence: 1-202-543-5566; www.nnedv.org

Asian & Pacific Islander Institute on Domestic Violence: 1-415-568-3315; www.apiidv.org

Eucuentro Latino National Institute on Family Violence: 1-888-743-7545; www.latinodv.org

National Immigrant Family Violence Institute: 1-314-773-9090, ext. 150; www.nifvi.org

Institute on Domestic Violence in the African American Community: 1-877-643-8222; www.idvaac.org

National Health Resource Center on Domestic Violence: 1-888-792-2873; www.futureswithoutviolence.org

Resource Center on Domestic Violence: Child Protection and Custody: 1-800-527-3223; www.nnedv.org/resources

Alianza: National Latino Alliance for the Elimination of Domestic Violence: 1-800-216-2404; www.dvalianza.org

Sacred Circle: National Resource Center to End Violence against Native Women: 1-877-733-7623; www.sacred-circle .com

Acknowledgments

As I read through my journals, I began to relive my experiences and came to the strong realization that the truth needed to be shared. Not only for me, but for the 4.8 million women in America who are abused each year, and the countless victims worldwide. I hope this book sheds light on how you can be innocently led into the cycle of abuse and not even realize it until it's too late. I want people to understand how extremely difficult it was for me to leave. It took me six years, four months, and twelve days. Over three million minutes, each one filled with love or fear . . . sometimes both.

I want abused women to get out, and I want those around them to be supportive until they find the courage to do so, no matter how long it takes.

My deepest love and gratitude goes out to those who supported me and continue to do so:

Kennedy—you give me a reason to live, love, and laugh. You are my whole world.

"Mimi" Taylor—for a lifetime of unconditional love. I love you.

Randall Taylor—thank you for my third and final name, and for becoming the dad I always wanted.

My grandmother—wish you were here. It's been twenty-seven years, and I have missed you every second of it.

Aunt Dianna—for inspiring me to dream, travel, and live the "big life."

Delena and Arlie—I've always known I can go home.

Dwight Coates—you never fail me.

Jennifer Diamond—ten ten forever and always.

Rick Walker—twenty-two years of laughter, jeez, you're getting old.

Dr. Charlie Sophy—for my voice and my life.

John Bluher—you fight the good fight, always. Deepest gratitude.

George Santo Pietro—I stopped "wallowing" in it because of you and my treasured wounds are finally healed. Grazie.

Acknowledgments

Francisco Martin—we went through it together. Mi familia.

Julie Waldorf Martin—sorbet scoops and hugs.

Elaine Culotti—for feeding me on Sundays and making things happen.

Gloria Perez—you protected and cared for us.

The Wives—what a roller coaster. We are bonded for life, like it or not!

Andy Cohen—you keep the hot seat hot and the clubhouse rockin'.

Francis Berwick—no one does it better . . . period.

Alex Baskin and Douglas Ross—for the opportunity, and for always editing me to look better than the other Wives. Wink wink.

Dave Rupel, Chris Cullen, Larry, Brenda—for Oprah lighting and the soft focus lens.

Julie Ritchie—you were there, thank you.

Josh Tatum—all those nights, sleepless nights.

Phil McGraw—for listening.

Acknowledgments

Stuart Goffman—a great sounding board and friend.

John Treace—my heart will never be the same.

Carol Adelkoff and Tobi Quintilianni—inspiration, always.

Robert Thorne—you managed to manage me even when I was unmanageable.

Greg Reditz—editor, whip cracker, and all around nice guy.

Terri Stump and Liz Ritchie—it wouldn't have been the same without back handsprings and ponytails.

Sarah Tomlinson—you made it all go together, seamlessly. Thank you for tolerating me . . . and my voice.

Jan Miller—savvy, sophisticated, and stylish. You went to bat and hit it out of the park.

Jen Bergstrom at Simon and Schuster—for believing my story was worth telling.

Linda Thompson—for always providing the voice of reason.